THAT HAMLET ON THE HILL
Remembering a former life in Somerset

THAT HAMLET ON THE HILL
Remembering a former life in Somerset

Stewart Seviour

Publisher: Stewart Seviour>
2018

First Printing: 2018

ISBN 978-0-244-08075-4

<

Contents

Acknowledgements..ix

Foreword xi

Introduction 1

Family Life..7

Family background 11

Moving to Stratton village 17

Infant and Junior school 1955-1961....................................29

Sheila Smith diaries of 1956...37

St Vigors school register excerpts 39

Moving to big school...41

Teenage years...51

Stratton village and Downside...55

Village institutions..61

Neighbouring areas 69

A nice gesture 77

A Great Train Robber in Stratton! 79

Stratton People Collection..81

Village football 83

Stratton cricket 87

The story of a record player 91

Part-time jobs 95

Starting work 99

Voluntary redundancy 119

Crossroads 125

Transport 133

Going back 137

How a junior typewriter got me to Spain! 139

Other titles by Stewart Seviour 142

Acknowledgements

I would like to thank all the people who have contributed to this book by supplying information, anecdotes and photographs. Especially helpful have been Nick James of D.H. James Photography Wells, and certain members of the Stratton-on-the-Fosse and Midsomer Norton History Photo Booth Facebook Pages.

Lynne Shaw, and my son Mark, have given invaluable assistance with proof reading, editing and grammar.

I dedicate this book to my late brother Colin Seviour, and to my late cousin Steve Seviour, both of whom passed away in 2016.

Foreword

How does anyone put their thoughts and memories to paper without the work seeming like an autobiography? To me, that is what someone rich or famous, or a person who has a particularly interesting tale to tell would write My intention was merely to record what it was like to be born and raised in a small rural village in the 1950's and 1960's, in the hope that it would perhaps be of interest to some readers.

There are many reasons why normal, everyday people wish to write their memoirs, and are often encouraged to do so, and possibly the current trend of researching ones family tree has something to do with this. On webpages such as Family Search and FreeReg it can be very rewarding and entertaining to chart various branches of your family, and I have managed myself to research as far back as 1750.

Pure nostalgia is one of the main reasons that people like to write their memoirs, and many of us like to turn the clock back occasionally. You only have to see how popular such tv shows as Talking Pictures and Shed and Buried are, and this latter program is the most successful one on the Travel Channel. We often regret the demise of those great British motorbikes for instance, such as Norton, Triumph and BSA, our manufacturing industries, or maybe we just miss some of the morals and values of our younger days. Photographs, people and places are never forgotten.

There are other reasons for writing your memoirs such as requests from family, or maybe because the writer still has a good long-term memory and prefers to pen them before his fingers get too arthritic, or before his eyesight fails too much! As well as the above motivations for writing, I would add my main one, which is the fact that I have not lived in Stratton-on-the-Fosse since 1972, and not lived in the UK since 1991, and although I would not say that I miss living there, I have never forgotten my roots, and have fond memories of them.

If Stratton-on-the-Fosse really is such a small hamlet, why bother writing about it at all? I think the last paragraph explains my reasons, but I know that we were fortunate to have been born and bred in such a pleasant area, and in a county that is diverse and steeped in history with so many famous cities and places to visit.

Hopefully, I will be excused for perhaps writing in excessive detail the passages on places of employment, and the descriptions of what it was like to have worked in them. I had thought of calling this book Rambling Around The Mendips, or Rambling Around Somerset, but feel that this would seem like I was writing about a walking tour. Instead, I think I have rambled enough with my keyboard!

Stewart Seviour. Málaga, Spain. April 2018

Introduction

Early in 2009, my wife and I were lucky enough to win a fantastic cruise to the Bahamas, and on disembarking in Miami a US Customs Officer was scrutinizing my UK passport. "Where is Stratton-on-the-Fosse?" he asked me interestedly. When I replied that it was a small village in Somerset, in the west country of England, he drawled, "Sounds very nice, like to go there myself one day." Well, I felt like saying, "Better not blink then, or you will miss it!"

Mr Wilmott, who was our old Deputy Headmaster at Somervale School, Midsomer Norton, probably thought the same thing. One year we were putting on a performance of A Midsummer Night's Dream, and not being too keen on Shakespeare or acting, I was given the role of understudy to Puck! On a particular evening I told him that I was not able to stay behind for rehearsals as my bicycle had a puncture, and that I would have to catch the bus home. He looked at me suspiciously and asked where I lived. "Stratton Sir," I told him.

"Ah yes, lad," he replied, "that little hamlet on the hill!"

Stratton really *is* more of a hamlet than a village, and the place where I was born in 1950 was not even inside of its borders; Norton Hall Cottages being a group of four stone-built dwellings surrounded by fields and accessible by a long drive. Officially or not, Norton Down and White Post were recognised as a part of Stratton-on-the-Fosse, and the cottages were owned by local landowner Louis Beauchamp. On reading the history of the coalfields in Britain, those of North Somerset do not seem to get mentioned as much as those in South Wales or Durham   for example, but many men from Somerset villages worked in the pits, my grandfather included.

NORTON HALL

Norton Hall had been built by 1674, when John Tooker lived there, a partner of John Salmon of Holcombe, they mined coal in Stratton.

James Tooker was High Sherrif of Somerset in 1766.

Hyde Whalley Salmon Tooker was the last of this family to live there.

The house was used by Frome Deanery school and in 1866 the occupant was Squire Thomas Purnell, a local wheelwright, coach builder and undertaker.

It is believed that when the railway was being built in 1874/1874, the labourers used the empty house for shelter. When Norton Hall was damaged by fire in the late 19th century, some wood panelling, stone and the iron gates were re-used locally.

Public domain information on Norton Hall.

I remember my grandparents living in Norton Down Cottages, and these dwellings are still standing today, although another rank nearby has long since been demolished. The cottages were small, with no mains electricity in those days, and the outside toilets were situated halfway down the very long gardens.

More than a few younger families from Norton Down moved up to Stratton village in the 1950's, but the only neighbours I remember living near my grandparents, were the Moggs. My Grandparents cottage was owned by (Jiggles) Orchard, and I was there one day when he came in for the rent money. Gran asked him how he was, as he was complaining as usual, and I heard him say, "Its me knee Missus, me bloody knee!"

Harry was a keen gardener, which ran in the family, as did an interest in wildlife. A species of bird nested in their garden for several years, so we looked it up and found it was a Spotted Flycatcher. When Grandad died, only our older cousins were allowed to his funeral, although from the bottom of the Bath View estate we could see his hearse parked outside of St Vigors church; an image that sticks in the mind of a 9 year old.

As still seems to be the custom today, a funeral service would be held in the Norton Down Methodist Chapel, followed by internment in St Vigor's churchyard. In fact, when the Norton Down Chapel was opened in 1888, the story goes that Methodists and Anglicans had shared use of the building by means of the east side in the mornings, and the west side in the evenings! It seems that before the chapel was built, worshippers used to congregate in the nearby cottages, and also in the White Post Inn. As pupils of St Vigors Church of England School, we attended Sunday school at Norton Down Methodist Chapel, which shows how the different faiths merged at that time! My memories are not all that clear, but Summers and Nash, the firm who delivered paraffin and household wares, seemed to be involved with the chapel. Gordon Summers certainly springs to mind as being one of our Sunday school teachers, and he may have been a lay minister there. We youngsters were a bit unruly, and it could have been the Nash family who had the job of controlling us! At the back of the chapel there was a piece of overgrown land where old furniture and such had been thrown, and I can remember a large harp being abandoned there which we would play with. A minibus from Alfords Coaches would pick us up and take us to Sunday school and back, and this was usually driven by a man called Albert. In those days of course, most mothers baked their own cakes, and we inevitably came home from Sunday school to a lovely tea which included a jam sponge or a plate of rock cakes!

Traffic wise, the White Post crossroads was a dangerous place in years gone by and countless accidents occurred there before a new roundabout was built. For years there was a yellow AA box standing on the opposite side of the road to the pub, and I can remember standing at the bus stop that used to be a fixture there. As far as I remember, Stratton was served by 2 bus routes, the 184 Bath to Frome which turned left at the war memorial and went on through Holcombe and Coleford, and the Bath to Shepton Mallet, which conveniently stopped outside of Bath View in Stratton. The White Post public house has changed over the years, as have all establishments that need to survive. As kids, we were never allowed inside a pub by law even accompanied, and very few places had facilities outside such as beer gardens. Don Woolfrey was the landlord at White Post for several years, and it was very much a place where darts, shove-halfpenny and cards were played. Larry Bush later ran a successful business there.

Going south from White Post to Stratton-on-the-Fosse, and on the brow of the hill, lies the area which has the captivating name of Killings Knap. How the name came about I am not sure of, but as Stratton lies roughly on the line of the old Roman Fosse Way, Roman remains have been found there. For years there stood a rank of red brick cottages at Killings Knap, and a family by the name of Weekes came to live there in the 1950's. On the opposite side of the Fosse Way is Killings Knap Farm which used to be owned by Russell Burnett, and later by one of Downside's teachers. During the tenancy of this master, Norman Andrews ran his leather works from an outbuilding there, before moving to permanent premises in Stratton village. I have memories of working on Norman's cutting press in the barn there, and being surrounded by chickens!

I think the large rubbish tip that was situated at Killings Knap was used by Downside, and I can recall Mr Hughes emptying his mauve coloured lorry there. Ashamedly to say, but as kids we would go to this tip looking for pram wheels for our trucks, and the site was an eyesore, so much so that when Prince Charles visited the area in his capacity as Duchy of Cornwall, the whole tip was bulldozed and landscaped!

Another landmark that has now disappeared, was the Downside glider shed which stood in the corner of the field just down from Stratton's football pitch. Nothing now exists either of the cottage that used to belong to the legendary Granny Green. Judy Green lived for years alone in this isolated stone cottage on the outskirts of Luckham Woods, and when we were young, there were still traces of the dwelling remaining. Gerald Green is a relative of Granny, and still lives in Stratton.

Another local legend that seems more fiction than fact, is the story that an American GI jeep lies at the bottom of Emborough Pond! There were of course many American servicemen stationed in Somerset during WW2, and between 1942 and 1945 the American military took over the running of Shepton Mallet Prison. Around 18 American military prisoners were executed there during that time, most of them being hanged by British executioners Albert and Thomas Pierrepoint. When Shepton Prison closed in 2013, it was the UK'S oldest operating one.

That Hamlet on the Hill

Stewart Seviour

Family Life

Unless you were a Roman Catholic, not many of our parents were regular churchgoers, but we were brought up as Christians and learned the Bible, and also the meaning of right and wrong. We observed all the festivals of the church, which we only really attended as school, or Sunday school pupils, but most families respected Good Friday for instance by not eating meat, and we were not allowed to have our Easter eggs until Easter Sunday! Christmas was a magical time, even though most families were poor, and in those days a chicken or cockerel for Christmas dinner was an annual treat. Mum made and iced her own Christmas cake, as well as mince pies and Christmas puddings that she would steam in the metal copper. My brother and sister and I would hang up a large sock or a pillowcase on the end of our beds, and wake up very early on Christmas morning to see what presents we had. One year I had an electric train set, but was disappointed as the transformer I needed to work it had not arrived, so I had to wait until after the holidays before I could use it. Cowboy outfits, jigsaw puzzles and conjuring outfits were favourite gifts for us boys, and when I was older I was given my first guitar. Christmas television programmes seemed to be much the same every year with a Laurel and Hardy film shown in the morning, or else that famous speeded up train journey from Paddington to Brighton in 4 minutes. This film was originally used by the BBC as an interlude between programmes in the days of live tv, but it thrilled us kids every time we saw it! Following the Queen's message after lunch, Billy Smarts or Chipperfields Circus was the usual fare dished up in the afternoon, with maybe a Disney cartoon as well. Boxing Day viewing was fairly predictable too, and who can forget those Brian Rix farces such as 'Dry Rot`, and the pantomimes with a woman playing the male lead, and a man dressed up as the main woman! As we were older, Boxing Day was the day to go out and have a drink with family and friends, and the first chance to use your new jumper and aftershave you had been given as presents! Lunch was normally the rest of the turkey in one form or another.

As a young child I cannot remember being very excited on New Years Eve or Valentine's Day, (that came later in life!) so probably the next event of the year was Shrove Tuesday or Pancake Day. I called it Pancakes Day as I used to eat more than one of them, and they were delicious with lemon and sugar! I can't remember us ever giving up anything for Lent, although I do remember someone once saying that they had given up making their bed in the morning!

We looked forward with anticipation to our birthdays, and usually had a tea party for our closest friends who would each bring you a present, often an Airfix model aeroplane, or a bag of assorted sweets that were all stuck together. When I was around 10 or 11 years old I told my parents that I would like a stopwatch for my birthday, and looking back now, having a wristwatch seemed unheard of in those days. It appealed to me that we could have running races and be timed, and we did this often in the fields that had been harvested, and still had the straight lines left by the mower. Anyway, I knew I was going to have the stopwatch as I happened to see it in mum's handbag a few days before my birthday!

Often for Christmas or birthdays we were given annuals, which were books with stories and pictures based either on tv programmes or comics. One year I was disappointed to be given a Rawhide annual by two different people! Favourite comics as youngsters included the Beano, Dandy and Beezer, and when I was older, I bought the Victor every week so that I could read about Alf Tupper winning athletic races after a eating a meal of fish and chips!

Stewart Seviour

During our teen years we became very aware and interested in the annual sports events, and were lucky to have been able to see many of them on normal BBC or ITV. We would be glued to the screen for the Boat Race every year between Oxford and Cambridge, and for the Grand National. As now, Wimbledon was shown for the whole fortnight, and us kids would make a makeshift net and court, and pretend to be Rod Laver or John Newcombe with our wooden rackets! England's football internationals were shown, or heard on the radio live in those days, with Kenneth Wolstenholme and David Coleman commentating, but my favourite sport was cricket, and especially the test matches. During the summer holidays we would watch cricket on BBC for hours on end, and then listen to the ball by ball commentary on the radio when we had to leave the house. Invariably England would get stuffed against Australia or West Indies, but the worst disappointment was when 'rain stopped play'.

That Hamlet on the Hill

Family background

My paternal grandfather Henry James (Harry) Seviour died in 1960 at the age of 72, and my scant memories of him were of a tall man with large hands who would say to me in a gruff voice, "Hello my old cocker!" He was born and lived all his life in and around White Post and Chilcompton, and I have seen photos of him as goalkeeper for the White Post football team that they had in his younger days. He was a miner for some of his working life, and my own father would tell me how grandad would ride to work and back on his bike, and often come home to a dinner of bread and jam. Apparently Harry's bike was a massive affair, and his mode of dismounting was by falling off it! Dad told me the story of when one day Harry had an accident. He rode to work round the lanes to Bristol Stone and Concrete in Holcombe with his mate, who happened to be late one morning, so decided to wait for him round a bend and up against the hedge. My granddad heard his mate peddling down the hill towards him and heard him shout out, "Be that you Harry?"

"Ah", he replied.

"Well bide there then," shouted out his mate, but instead of staying where he was, Harry pushed his bicycle out into the road where the two men collided!

"Be that blood?" asked my worried granddad, feeling his wet coat.

"No, that's tea Harry ya silly bugger, has't broke thee flask!"

White Post football team 1919-20. Goalkeeper Harry Seviour is middle back row (Courtesy of Penny Seviour)

My paternal grandmother Blanche was also from White Post, and belonged to the large family of Whittocks. The story goes that her brothers were drinkers and often fought between themselves, so that when she was married and lived next door she got her husband Harry to go round and "sort them out!" Blanche died early in the 1980's, and I believe she was around 89 years old. I have very fond memories of Gran who was a very sweet person and never offended anyone. I can remember her coming to visit us as kids in Bath View, and she would nearly always bring a tin of pilchards for my brother! When I was married with children she would come to tea and always insisted on washing the dishes afterwards.

My father Edward John – Ted to everyone, was born at White Post in 1919. He had an elder brother Jim, and a younger sister Olive. As teenagers, Jim and Ted were keen amateur boxers, and fought each other on occasions. Ted was called up when war broke out in 1939 and joined the Wiltshire Regiment, while Jim saw service with the Home Guard. Dad was sent to several places for training, including Basingstoke in Hampshire, and it was here that he met my mother Violet Elsie Thomson, as she was. Mum was born in 1916 to a large family of 7. Her father was Scottish, and had been a railway worker, but although I think I met him once when I was very small, only remember him from photos.

My father saw service with The Royal Welch Fusiliers in India and Burma, and was demobbed in 1945 as corporal, having also served in the Military Police.

Military Police in India: Ted Seviour back row second left.

During the last year or so of the war while dad was abroad, my mother spent her holidays in Somerset, staying with my grandparents at Bennell Cottages in Chilcompton before going back to work in a munitions factory. Olive was married by this time and also stayed with her parents while her husband Eric was away fighting. Mum and dad were married early in 1946, and not long afterwards moved to Norton Hall Cottages where they were living when my sister Pat was born in 1947 on Dad's 28th birthday.

After leaving school at age 14, dad had started work at Bristol Stone and Concrete in Holcombe, and after being demobbed from the army resumed his job there. Brother Jim and my grandfather were also employed at the same place by this time. One condition of his rental agreement at Norton Hall was that he was obliged to help out with the haymaking every summer. In those difficult days after the war there were advantages to living in the countryside though, and no doubt many a rabbit was poached to supplement a poor table!

My memories of living at Norton Down are naturally poor as I was only 4 when we left there to live in Stratton proper, but I do remember the day we moved. My father and I were standing at the bottom of the garden, waiting for a lorry to arrive to transport our furniture to our new home in Bath View. I can remember saying to him, "That's the one," and it was indeed a grey lorry from Bristol Stone that was driven by Jack Howard. There was a large hump near where we were standing, but I did not realise at the time that this was the air raid shelter the neighbours shared during the war. I doubt that it was ever used, not for the purpose it was meant for anyway.

Other vague memories are of walking across the fields at the back of the house to where the Somerset and Dorset Railway ran. This was in a deep cutting just before the trains entered Chilcompton Tunnel, after having come from Midsomer Norton.

Harry & Blanche Seviour with children and neighbours.
White Post around 1930. Courtesy of Penny Seviour

Our neighbours at Norton Down were the Bodmin's, and Bill the father worked on the farm. They were a large and friendly family, and I know my parents kept in touch with them for many years after we had left. In the early 60's when I started a part-time job delivering bread for Steam Mills Bakery of Midsomer Norton, it was Mrs Bodmin who recommended me, and it was nostalgic for me to go back up that long drive and to have her as a customer. Years later, Steam Mills were to hold other nostalgic memories for me when we started to run a corner shop nearby.

My late younger brother Colin was also born at Norton Hall on Boxing Day 1953, and it must have seemed fantastic for the family to move to a 3 bedroomed council house the following year, complete with mains electricity and water!

Many years later Norton Hall Cottages were purchased and converted for some years into a private residential home.

That Hamlet on the Hill

Moving to Stratton village

Bath View, built around 1953, was a modern council estate of some forty five 2 and 3 bedroomed semi-detached and terraced houses, which years later were proved to be of doubtful quality when some of the tenants had the option to purchase their homes. We lived in number 30, which was a corner plot with large gardens, although these were severely restricted later on when garages were built on some of that land. Our immediate neighbours were an elderly couple the Germains, and Frank had worked at Chilcompton railway station as a porter, as had another near neighbour Mr (Smudger) Smith. On the other side of us lived the Perrett family, and the father Tony was quite a local celebrity!

Left: Shaun Delaney & Eamonn Andrews in Whats my Line.

Another temporary famous Bath View resident was Shaun Delaney, who was employed at Downside School as a tuck shop assistant. He appeared on BBC's What's My Line, although his occupation was soon guessed by panel member Gilbert Harding!

Although money was short for most families, we had a happy childhood in Stratton, and through living in the countryside obviously spent a lot of time outdoors. The local farmer Cliff Perkins would let us use part of a large field we called Cattlegate as a football and cricket pitch, and us kids would build a large bonfire there for Guy Fawkes Night. All the fields around us had names; Cattlegate, The Cradle, Two Ponds, The Dip etc. and they were all logical names due to their features. Most of us were football and cricket mad, and we would take our fathers lawn mowers to Cattlegate to cut the grass! Cradle field was fantastic for sledging when we had snow, and that seemed to be every winter in those days. We really did enjoy the countryside, and would build dens in the trees and hedges, hang swings from tall branches, go bird nesting, pick mushrooms and play doctors and nurses with the girls! Sometimes we would go farther afield to scrump apples from Countess De Salis'estate, or to pick mushrooms from Downside cricket field, (often to be chased off by their groundsman Wilf Bendell). Luckham Woods was also a favourite haunt for us Stratton kids. Mostly though I guess we grew up in an innocent, protected environment compared with nowadays.

Bath View in the 1960's, with cricket wicket in the field to the right. Mr Di Maggio's black cobblers shed is in far right corner plot.
(Courtesy of D.H. James Photography)

To the west of Bath View were the so-called Smith´s Houses as can be seen on the left of the photo. These private houses were nicknamed because Harry Smith from Smiths Bakery lived in one of them, and may have even owned more of them. The wall at the bottom of their long gardens was also our boundary wall until the garages were built in Bath View. The top of that wall was tarred and had broken glass to keep us kids from retrieving our lost footballs! Local metalworker Bill Bolton lived at one time in the Smiths house at the front of the photo, and worked from the long shed/garage facing the field. I once asked Bill if he could repair a split I had in the petrol tank of my motorbike.

"You must be joking," he replied, "that´s dangerous, I

What was Bath View, is now a modern estate.

would have to drain and wash out the tank, fill it with sand, then leave it for weeks before I could touch it." I was going to walk away disappointed when he added, "Bring it round tomorrow and I will weld it!" I did, and there was no explosion!

Another interesting family that moved to one of the Smith houses were the Knotts, who hailed from the Timsbury or Temple Cloud area. The family were steeplejacks, and both my brother-in-law and a friend were employed by them at one time, working on church and building restoration. I knew the Knotts to have one daughter, and the father and four sons were all steeplejacks. Opposite Bath View and on Downside land, were some very tall and straight pine trees, and one day we saw one of the younger Knott brothers scale right up to the top of one of them quickly and with ease, to what must have been at least 100 feet.

A former Bath View resident, Franco Di Maggio, has been immortalized in the Radstock Museum. In the garden of a corner plot stood a dark coloured shed, and this was where Franco Di Maggio conducted his cobblers business. Franco came to Britain from Italy in 1950, recruited to be a coal miner on a 2 year contract, but met his wife and obtained permission to stay. Mr Di Maggio had an excellent reputation for repairing footwear, and gained many customers from Stratton and whereabouts.

Stratton cobbler Franco Di Maggio.
(Courtesy of Maria Mitchell)

Several Italians settled in Stratton during the 1950′s and 60′s, but unlike Mr Di Maggio, they mostly came over to work at Downside. One gentleman I remember well was Nino Ludovici, as he became the village barber, operating from a shed in gardens that used to be opposite the post office. Nino was a good barber, but as a kid I dreaded going to him as I could not stand the smell of garlic on his breath!!

As boys, we also visited Fred Hale who was a barber in Chilcompton, and who also carried out his business from a converted garden shed. On occasions though we would cycle to Midsomer Norton with dad to get our haircuts at either Stan Ashman or Glenn Phillips. Often we would have to buy spare parts or accessories for our cycles, and in those days we went to Toveys in the High Street. On the return journey we would have to push our bikes up Silver Street and under the old railway bridge, then mount again to ride up the lane to Norton Down where my gran lived in one of the cottages there. She would often give us a cup of tea and fried potato sandwiches.

Although there were shops in the village, not many families had cars in the 50′s and 60′s to travel far afield, hence there were countless delivery companies. Both Smiths and Steam Mills delivered bread by van from Mondays to Saturdays, as did the Coop. There were several firms delivering milk every morning, including local Farmer Padfield who drove round the village with a trailer on his car, often assisted by young Teddy Wilson. Strawbridge Butchers from Chilcompton called a couple of times a week, and our parents bought their joints and sausages from their Stratton born employee John Bendle. I can recall a man we used to call ′Yes Madam` selling wet fish from his van, usually on a Friday morning, and during the summer holidays we would look forward to the Corona lorry coming to Bath View. Soft drinks at home were usually homemade lemonade, or orange squash that you had to dilute with water, so Corona′s fizzy drinks were a real treat. The highlight of our week though was Wednesday evenings when Stan

Brewer from Coleford called with his mobile shop. Stan sold practically everything you would get from a grocers or sweetshop, but in the early days before regulations came in, he would also sell fireworks to us kids in the weeks leading up to Bonfire Night. Before the time when we children in the estate erected a large fire in Cattlegate every November, most families would have their own bonfire in their garden, where they would let off their own fireworks. It makes you shudder now when you think of the things we would do, such as holding bangers as they went off, or leaning over to light the fuses on the rockets!

There were so many other delivery vans who called on a regular basis, not least of all the ice-cream men; Walls, Verrachios, Mr Whippy etc. and I believe there used to be a Mr Taylor who was an independent ice-cream man. At one time there was even a mobile fish and chip that used to call, but this later suffered a fire. Paraffin and other household items were delivered by the 'Oilmen' Summers and Nash and Harold Shearn. At one time (Whitey) White used to call every fortnight, and as young kids it was always a bit of a mystery who he actually was, but I believe our mothers bought clothes from him and paid in instalments – a Tallyman. A mobile library was a very much appreciated service, and I would imagine it was sent out from either Radstock or Midsomer Norton. One of our main callers though was the Coop van, or to be precise, the Radstock Cooperative Society mobile delivery shop. Their cream coloured van was large enough to carry a shopful of stock, and I can remember my mother mostly buying tinned goods

Top: Coop Van. (Courtesy of Kevin Chard)
Bottom: Same van in Stratton early 1960's

from the van. A member posted this photo of the van on a Midsomer Norton Facebook page, and asked if anyone could remember it. Some time later while looking through some old photographs, I found the following one of my brother and I taken in Bath View around the late 1950's or early 1960's, and with the same van in the background! Kevin tells me that his father and grandfather were the drivers of the van.

That Hamlet on the Hill

The coalman was a very important person too, as most houses were heated by solid fuel. Several coal merchants called at Stratton over the years, and Perkins is one name I remember. Another delivery man who worked for a different firm was nicknamed 'Wyatt Earp` by us for some reason! All of our houses had a concrete built outbuilding, with a portion of it as the coal bunker. The coalman emptied his sack there; the coal usually coming in largish lumps, so it was often my job to break them up with a lump hammer to fill the skuttle. Our dads had tools for everything in those days, lump hammers, clawhammers to pull out nails, and ordinary hammers to knock them in with! Our house was heated by just a coal fire in the living room which gave off a nice heat if you were sat in front of it, but as it had no effect on the other rooms, you went to bed frozen! After my sister got married and left home I took over her north-facing bedroom, which had its windows iced up for most of the winter. In the kitchen there was a Rayburn which also used coal, so this room and its airing cupboard were always warm at least. The Rayburn had a back boiler to heat the water, as well as an oven and hotplate to cook on. To compliment coal, which was expensive, we would often burn chumps of wood on the living room fire as they were a very effective and cost saving fuel. Mostly we got the chumps as off cuts from Sheppards sawmill in Chilcompton, which used to be situated on the road going down to the railway station. Dad and I, and sometimes my brother would ride our bikes over to Sheppards, fill up coal sacks with the chumps, then freewheel back across the bridle path with them hanging over our crossbars it being impossible to pedal like that. Another cost saving way of heating your house was by picking up coal from the local slag heap at New Rock Colliery. This was prohibited of course, but nonetheless it was not uncommon for the heads of the house to go out early in the morning to pick a sackful of slag!

As rather an isolated community with little or no facilities, we made our own entertainment and took an interest in outsiders. In the early years before Bath View became quite shabby, painters would come round to paint all the doors and

Local painter & Decorator Arthur Ladd.
(Courtesy of Marlene Maggs)

window frames, and would even creosote our garden gates. If I remember correctly, Ladds were the firm who were contracted, and most of the girls on the estate fancied the son Nigel!

In those days dustbins were just that, made of galvanize to hold the ashes and dust from coal fires, although the cinders were also put on the gardens and paths. Residents had to put their dustbin out on the pavement every week for the dustman, or refuse collector to empty, and during the summer holidays we kids would carry the bins back to some of the houses, hoping that we would be given a tip.

One of my favourite memories was of helping out with the haymaking in Farmer Perkins fields. Originally the hay was combed up with a large rake on the front of the tractor, then loaded on to an elevator with pitchforks to make a rick. Later on though when we were teenagers, balers were introduced, and we would help pick up the bales of hay and load them on to the tractor and trailor, sitting on top of them on the journey back to the farm. Farmers used to help each other in those days, and often Russell Burnett and Derek Candy from adjoining farms would assist Cliff Perkins. Funnily enough though, I can never remember any association with Stratton's other farmer Mr Padfield. Farmer Perkins only had one son, who I think was in the navy, but several daughters, some of whom helped out. The sisters are still a very close knit family, and meet up with each other most weeks. Nigel Curtis and I had helped out for several days, but after haymaking was over could not see any pay forthcoming, so decided to call at the farm to ask. It took a couple of disrupted trips before we picked up courage though, and eventually knocked the door. Farmer Perkins answered himself and luckily knew what we wanted, so he paid us both according to our ages!

Television was new to us in the 1950's, and most households still only had BBC. Near neighbours the Cullen family were one of the first to have ITV, and my earliest recollections are of watching Popeye cartoons, and seeing the Pepsodent toothpaste adverts! You could tell which house had ITV or BBC by the aerial on their roof, which would be the original H shape, or a later X one.

Those tv westerns and series of the 1950's and 60's had a big effect on us kids, and they spawned many fashion fads and gimmicks. I have been a lifelong fan of tv westerns, and most of us boys had holsters and pistols which shot caps that either came in a roll or individually. Its a pleasure to still be able to see some of the old episodes of Rawhide, Wagon Train and The Virginian on Youtube. We have lost a few of the western heroes recently such as Ty Hardin (Bronco) Hugh O'Brian (Wyatt Earp) and Dale Robertson (Wells Fargo) who all lived to be in their eighties and nineties. Robin Hood of course has a special place in English folklore, and the series starring Richard Greene as Robin and Alan Wheatley as the Sheriff of Nottingham was very popular and must have sent sales of bows and arrows flying! We made our own however by choosing a nice straight hazel stick from the hedge, then bending it over and attaching the string to both ends. The arrows we made in the same way, and I can even remember making points for them with pieces of broken old 78 records, and storing them in a quiver made by mum! William Tell was another favourite tv series starring Conrad Phillips, but as crossbows were a bit difficult to make yourself, both wooden and metal ones, complete with rubber suckered darts, were all the go for a while in toyshops. Other passing fads were Davy Crockett hats with a tail, and homemade Ivanhoe swords. It is surprising too that many of the catch phrases from old tv shows have never been forgotten by my generate.n, just recently I was playing petanca with friends and asked one of them what the score was, "Ten Four," she replied, prompting a chorus of "Over and out," from the rest of us, thinking of old Broderick Crawford as Cpt. Dan Matthews in Highway Patrol! And what about the bingo callers who shout out, "77 – Sunset Strip!"

Lots of us boys had homemade trucks or trolleys, and we were always on the lookout for pram wheels, even going to the local dump in search of them. I can remember having one new bicycle as a child, but mostly we built our own from parts and spares. The most important part of course was the frame, and a gents one rather than a ladies. We would rub it down, and hang it up in the shed from the ceiling to paint. We did not have spray paints in those days, so our brushwork left a lot to be desired. Handlebars, saddles, wheels and tyres etc. were either used from other bikes, or purchased from Tovey´s or Maggs in Midsomer Norton. Chequered tape, speedometers, three speed gears and horns were all accessories used at one time or another. We were always changing our handlebars from ´drops` to ´cowhorns` to ´butterflies` and a favourite trick was to tape a lolly stick to the frame so that it rattled against the spokes to make a motorbike sound!

Hula hoops, stilts and roller skates all had their day, but music lasted forever! We would buy our 45rpm vinyls and LP's mostly from Parsons shop in the Island in Midsomer Norton, and my first ever purchase was in 1962 when I bought Mr Guitar Man by Duane Eddy for my sister's birthday! The sale of 45's, or singles, were what the Hit Parade was based on, and we would faithfully listen to Alan Freeman playing the new Top Twenty every Sunday afternoon. Vinyls will buckle of course if subject to heat, and that is just what happened to one of my sister's records when I left it in the sun. I can still remember the name of it too – Butter Fingers by Tommy Steele!

Infant and Junior school 1955-1961

I started school when I was 5 years old at St Vigors C of E School, and our teacher in the infants class was Mrs Mears, who lived in Peasedown. The junior class was run by Headmistress Mrs Willis, a kindly woman who was married to a German ex serviceman Peter. Being a church school, we had visits every week from our vicar Mr Tunnell, and I can remember some winters we used to have snowball fights with him in the playground. My parents were not especially religious in that they attended church regularly, but they did bring us up as Christians. I was actually baptized in the Methodist Chapel at White Post, but then presumably became an

St Vigors School 1960-61. Mrs Mears is on the left and headmistress Mrs Willis on the right. The author is back row fifth from the left.

Anglican! It seemed that you followed whichever faith had the nearest church to where you lived, unless you were a Catholic of course, which I became many years later.

That Hamlet on the Hill

Our education at St Vigors was basic to say the least, and I can only remember one person ever passing his 11 plus examination to go to Grammer School at Midsomer Norton. I was good at reading and writing, spelling etc. and was told that I had narrowly missed out on passing my own 11 plus. When I started secondary school at Somervale at Midsomer Norton in 1961 I was put in the top A stream, but some of us soon found out that we were way below the standard of pupils from other primary schools such as Radstock Road and St Johns. I held my own quite well and stayed in A stream except for mathematics, which I struggled with.

At St Vigors we had no playing fields, only a small playground, so did not officially play football or cricket as lessons as many other junior schools did. We had other sports including rounders and netball, and gym equipment to take outside such as vaulting horses, medicine balls, bean bags etc. Every summer we had a sports day in the playground where we would take part in the usual races; egg and spoon, sack, three legged etc. and of course tug-of-war!! Playground games included 'off ground touch`, 'drop the hanky` and 'What's the time Mr Wolf`. Certainly there was bullying too between the older and younger pupils, but we regarded this as all part of growing up.

Our school day started, if I remember, at 9am, and in the junior class we would say prayers and sing hymns to Mr Willis' piano. It was on Thursday mornings that we would go round the class choosing a hymn to sing, and then continue taking turns the following Thursdays. On one of my turns I asked Mrs Willis for "Hills of the North Rejoice" which I liked, and she reluctantly played it saying something like, "Oh Stewart, that one is difficult." We all fell about laughing one morning though when one boy, I think his name was Stranks asked for 'Sugar in the Morning`. I am not sure if our headmistress had heard of that famous Alma Cogan hit of the day, or not, but she had to gently explain to Stephen that it wasn't a hymn!!

Like most village schoolrooms at the time, the only form of heating we had was a coke-burning stove which burned red hot around its base, but hardly gave out much heat unless you were close to it. On cold winter mornings we had to do exercises to get warm, jumping on the spot, shaking our fingers etc. A coke monitor was chosen every year, and he would go outside to fill the scuttle with coke so that the stove could be topped up. We also had ink monitors to fill the inkwells on all the desks, and milk monitors who would distribute the free third of a pint bottles to everyone. The three R´s formed the nucleus of our learning; we were taught how to join up our letters and learnt how to write essays, or ´compositions` as they were known to us. Storytelling and reading helped our spelling, and tests were given at the end of every school year. We started off arithmetic by learning our times tables, and the sing song way that this was taught to us proved to be a very effective method.

Geography and History were, I suspect, taught from an imperialist, protestant viewpoint, and considering the time and place, why not? We were encouraged to draw and paint, and I remember that our painting materials were kept in an old, wooden cupboard at the back of the classroom. Paints were in powder form which we had to mix up with water, and the cupboard always had an unpleasant smell when you opened it. Raffia work was another craft that boys as well as girls had to do, but my finished place mats were never a pretty sight to see! I am not sure what the subject would be called these days, but I enjoyed our lessons about nature. All the seasons of the year were covered, as we would plant hyacinth and crocus bulbs, then plot their growth and progress throughout the Spring and beyond. It was a great pleasure to go on nature walks with our teachers, and depending on the time of year, we would bring back flowers to press, as well as acorns, ´helicopter wings`, fir cones and hazel nuts to study.

There were annual outings to the seaside every year, to Weston-Super-Mare for the infants, and Weymouth for the juniors.

A Fry's coach from the village would be waiting on the road between the war memorial and the reading room, and pupil's families and friends could pay to come on the day out. As a boy, it always gave me a strange feeling to be sat in a coach waiting to travel somewhere. It was as if one was disorientated and not familiar with the surroundings you passed every day! The first thing we noticed was the coach, and secondly its driver! Fry's Coaches were established in Stratton-on-the-Fosse, and at one time had a stable of coaches and drivers taking customers on both local and continental journeys.

To put it in a nutshell, we kids were glad if we had a youngish driver and a smart, modern coach, but were not so keen if we had poor old Tommy Atkins and one of the older coaches! Anyway, we would always stop at Yeovil on the way to Weymouth, and the custom was to buy cherries there to eat on the coach. In those days most families took packed lunches to eat on the beach, and I can still remember now eating egg sandwiches with sand and grit in them. On the journey back, a stop was made at a pub in Castle Cary so that the adults could have a drink, and us youngsters a lemonade and a packet of crisps. Before the stop most people were tired and quiet, but on boarding the coach again singing would break out with 'Ten Green Bottles' 'Knees up Mother Brown' and other songs. As we were nearing home someone would take off his cap and go round to all the passengers to collect coins for the driver.

We celebrated all the Christian festivals, and the whole school would go down the road to St Vigor's Church at Christmas, Easter and Ascension Day, when we would be given the rest of the day off. Harvest Festival was special, and most of the kids would bring in vegetables and fruit that their parents had grown, while others would supply homemade cakes etc. All the produce was displayed in the church, and then, after the service was over it would be taken back to school and sold in aid of school funds. At Christmas we would have a carol service in the church, and the older pupils were expected to sing. For a couple of years I was one of the Three Kings, and Mrs Willis made me sing the most sombre verse ´Myrrh is Mine´, because she said that I always looked serious and worried! When we held a school play one year, she also cast me as the executioner.... Christmas parties were held every year in the school, with each pupil receiving a present, and I think it was in 1958 when we held a special party for the school´s 100 years anniversary.

Living and going to school in a small village meant that we were able to walk home for lunch, which was from midday to one o´clock, but school dinners were also available. Our next door neighbour Mrs Germain would very often meet my brother and I coming home with the same question, "Did ee get the stick today?" I´m not sure if she was kinky, or just thought that kids got the cane every day as they did in her time! Certainly my dad told me that he ´got the stick` his very first day at St Vigors. Apparently he clumped through the junior classroom disturbing the pupils, while wearing a pair of odd and very heavy boots, one brown and one black!

It seems funny looking back how naive we were as kids, and sometimes were not on the same wavelength as our elders. During one lesson our teacher asked us if we could recite any popular sayings such as, "Don´t do as I do, do as I tell you," etc. I put my hand up and said that I knew one. "Go on then," replied Mrs Willis, so I stood up and said,

"You make more noise that a boatful of sprats!" We were with the big class, and everyone went quiet all of a sudden, then Mrs Willis said, "I do not think I have heard that one before Stewart!" Of course, what I should have said was,

"You have more mouth that a boatload of sprats!"

It was on one of the days when we were individually called to the front of the class for a reading test, that Mrs Willis suspected that I was short sighted. For a long time I found it difficult to read the writing on the blackboard, but was afraid to say anything. I would squint my eyes, and even drop a pencil on the floor to try to see the board, and when I was told that I needed to wear glasses, it felt as though the bottom had fallen out of my life. In those days spectacles were round and basic, and there is no doubt that having to wear them restricted your life both physically and psychological. From then on it was an annual eye test at Adams and Edwards, who were at Stones Cross in those days before moving to their present location in Midsomer Norton. The optician Harry Edwards would put you at ease though, and when he retired it was his son who would be saying, "One, two, or better without", when testing the different strength lens on you.

Our family doctor was also based in Midsomer Norton, he was Dr Bulleid who had his surgery in The Dymbro, and who had been an army surgeon during the war. In those days your doctor would visit you at home, and follow this up with another to see how you were progressing. One summer I had been bedridden with mumps or measles or some other ailment, and when Dr Bulleid called a second time to see how I was progressing, my mother had to tell him that I was now better and had gone out helping with the haymaking! Very often though we would visit his surgery, usually when one of us had tonsillitis, and it seemed as though we were sat for hours in that waiting room on the hard, polished wooden benches, staring at the white wall tiles. Eventually the door would be opened and a voice would call out "Next". The doctor would ask you your name, and then take your index card out of his filing cabinet. "Stewart Seviour, doctor", I would say. "What is wrong with you Seviour?", he would reply, looking at you gravely over his spectacles. When Dr Bulleid retired, he was replaced by Dr Tucker who was a very nice person, and the practice was transferred to his house in North Road. Mrs Tucker was a pleasant woman too, and I believe she was Swedish. I was informed that Dr Tucker played the organ in church, including occasionally in the Old Church at Holcombe.

St. Vigors School photo 1957 with Mrs Willis and Mrs Mears,
(Courtesy of Pat Hand)

By the time my children were teenagers Dr Miller had taken over the practice, along with other GPs and in a new surgery.

That Hamlet on the Hill

Sheila Smith diaries of 1956

For anyone who has not read these fascinating diary excerpts, they are available on the Stratton-on-the-Fosse webpage at strattonpc.org

In October of 1956, Sheila and her colleague were student teachers from Bath University,and were sent to St Vigor's school to carry out geographical and environmental studies. Sheila gave permission for what remains of her studies to be published, in the form of her diary entries. Parts of the diary entries are hilarious, and her impressions of Stratton and its inhabitants of that time are extremely accurate. I would have only been 6 years old at the time and in the infants school, so obviously do not remember her visits, although I can recognize many of the pupils, parents, teachers and village people whom she wrote about. I read her diary entries after I started writing this book, and it was both exciting to have some of my own impressions and recollections confirmed, and instructive to learn about the day to day happenings in the school involving pupils up to 5 years older than me.

I also found it very interesting to read that Sheila had felt firsthand the religious divide in the village at that time. What I would not necessarily agree with, is her comment that maybe the youngsters felt this difference between Protestants and Catholics more that the older people. Certainly as schoolchildren we did not mix too much unless we were close neighbours, but as we grew older and started to socialize in the village, then religious bigotry hardly existed. Sheila was also correct in saying that some of the Downside boys looked down their noses at us village youths, although that would have been through reasons of class rather than of religion. I well remember one Sunday afternoon when a group of us village boys were sat on the war memorial (which we probably should not have been doing) when two Downside boys rode past on bicycles. One of the college boys shouted out ´peasants´ to us, which infuriated one of our number, who ran after them, and punched the outspoken one in the back! The Downside boy stopped and said, "If you would like a fight, I would be delighted to give you one", then quickly rode off! It was lucky for him that he did, as our friend was a quiet type, but tough as nails. He courted, and later married a girl from Peasedown, being not at all afraid of meeting her in the hometown of a gang of youths who were hostile towards us for a different incident.

Other interesting comments of Sheila´s that I can relate to concern her opinion of the then landlord of the Kings Arms pub, and of the aggressive attitude of some of the nuns who taught at St Benedicts School. As an outsider, she caught the general ambience of Stratton in the 1950´s, and the mien of some of its inhabitants. From her eye, she recognized how dreary winter was in a small village, but also how pleasant rural life could be in spring and summer. Sheila shrewdly weighed up certain of the village characters and pupils, spotting some of the cases of poverty and illiteracy that existed at the time, and even suggested interbreeding as a cause. The majority of the people she came into contact with though impressed her with their astuteness and friendliness, and also by the   kindness they had shown her after their original shyness.

St Vigors school register excerpts

On a visit to Somerset in 2015, I was thrilled to see an exhibition of old documents and photographs on show in Chilcompton village hall, and these included the register book from St Vigors School which is now available in the public domain. I found it fascination to read some of the excerpts from the register, including details of which pupils had left each year to go to secondary school, school equipment that had been purchased etc. and most of all, I was amazed to see the list of pupils going back several years. The students dates of birth are shown, and these go back to 1937 and beyond. It was intriguing to see names in the register of children born in say 1944 and 1945, because they would have been the eldest ones in the school when I started in 1955, and they probably bullied us!!

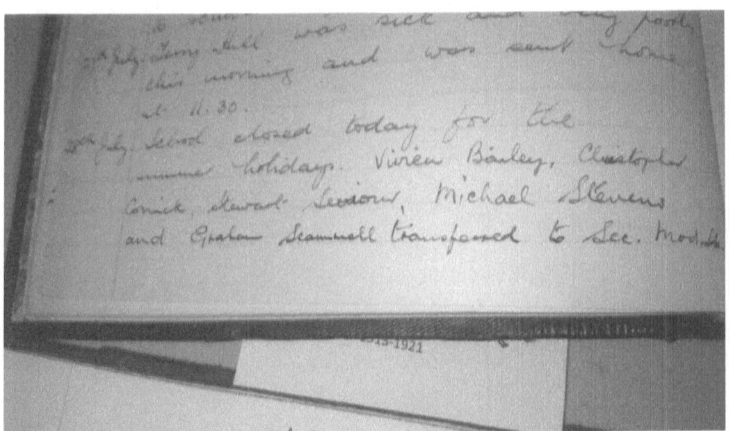

From St Vigors school register of 1961. Five of us left that summer.

That Hamlet on the Hill

Moving to big school

At age 11, most Catholic children from Stratton went on to Cardinal Newman Secondary School in Bath, later named St Gregorys, while the majority of Protestant ones who did not make it to Grammer school attended either Somervale Secondary Modern in Midsomer Norton., or the one at Writhlington.

Changing from primary to secondary school is always going to be worrying and even traumatic for many children, and the rumours going the rounds about how 'tough' life was at Somervale, and how new pupils were 'put in the dustbins' etc. did not make it any easier. One keen advantage on reaching 11 years old however was that you then had an extended summer holiday of 6 weeks and 2 days, instead of the 5 weeks at primary school! This was when we did our own bit of bullying at playtimes, by looking over our old school wall at the kids whose holidays were over, while we were still 'free'. We gloated and shouted at our juniors in the playground, in the same way that others had done to us previously, that was until Mrs Mears had to come and chase us away. Our day of reckoning was not far off though, and on the Wednesday of that seventh week we would be not so happy and carefree!

Moving on to secondary education was a real eye opener and cultural shock in many ways. For a start we had to wear a uniform for the first time, and this consisted of (for boys) a black blazer and grey trousers, with a green and yellow tie and breast pocket badge. Morning assemblies, timetables and lessons that we had never before experienced, such as gym, sports, woodwork and metalwork were all a big wake-up. We had never had male teachers at Stratton school, except for the occasional relief, so when I saw our new headmaster walk onto the stage before a hushed assembly, wearing a black gown and mortarboard, I felt like I wanted to run home to my mother! Discipline was strict too, and in those days most headmasters used the cane.

That Hamlet on the Hill

Our first year form teacher at Somervale was Mr Howell, and Chris is now a well known local author and historian. In later years we had Mr Edmonds and Mrs Grist. During 1961 Somervale's Sports Master Mr (Taffy) Johns was away, presumably on a course, so we had a Mr James for that first year. We never did play too much cricket at Somervale, and did not really have a school team. I remember once I went out to bat and took my stance, bat behind my feet and back straight, head up. The bowler was just about to run up when Mr Johns shouted "Stop, where did you learn to stand like that boy." I told him at Downside, as we village boys were allowed to play in the nets there after the pupils had gone home for their summer holidays. A few years later Len Johns went to Downside himself as Sports Master, to train

Happily retired teachers Mr & Mrs Johns with the author 2010

pupils much more apt than we were! Although us younger boys were rather in awe of ´Taffy` Johns, who was a strapping Welsh ex-rugby player, he did have a great sense of humour, and on wet days when it was impossible to go on the playing fields he would tell us stories, like the one about parking his car in a barn full of chickens and taking it out later covered in white spots! I remember my mother coming to one of our sports days and saying that Mr Johns had ´nice legs´. We boys hardly thought he was nice though, when we were forced to walk all the way up to White City in Welton to play football. This occurred when our own football pitch at Somervale was waterlogged and unplayable, and it would take us two whole lesson to walk to the substitute pitch and back again, leaving just half an hour or so for the game. White City was very open and exposed, and bitter cold, so the worst part was when we had to change into our clothes again. With frozen hands, we were given just a few minutes by 'Taffy' to get changed, under the threat of feeling his gym sole. On one occasion I had suffered an upset stomach, so my mother had to write the obligatory letter asking for me to be let off of games for that day. Unfortunately, she couldn't spell diarrhoea, so after a few misspelt attempts diarh... diahar... etc. she finally wrote that I had hurt my back! Much later, Mrs Johns was also teacher to my daughter and son at St Benedicts School.

At Somervale, our Headmaster Mr Rimmer would take us for the occasional lesson, and he would get us involved in interesting discussions and points of view. I remember one day he came into the class and we all stood up as normal. He started to point at 4 or 5 of us and said, "I envy you, and you, and you...," and then explained that he wished he wore spectacles as we did, as he would love to be able to take them off and hold them when he was talking etc. as a kind of prop! I hated wearing them, there were no contact lens in those days of course, and glasses used to be the round ugly National Health ones.

One of my favourite teachers was Mr Barber who took us for Biology, and it was his job to teach us the 'facts of life.' Mr Barber lived in Mells, and rode to school on his BSA Bantam motorcycle. Both in his choice of transport and his hobbies such as ornithology, he was not unlike my dad, and Mr Barber had also served his country in WW2. Often he would spend the whole of two lessons telling us of his wartime experiences, although I think he exaggerated sometimes with many of his tales. Around the early 1960's there were several cases of people being bitten by adders in the local beauty spot of Priddy, near Wells, and Mr Barber told us that he and some friends walked through the undergrowth there in wellington boots, which were later covered yellow with snakebite serum! Apparently, this teacher had one of the largest collections of birds eggs in the country, but woe betide anyone he knew of who had robbed a nest to get any themselves.

Mr Willmott and Miss Medlock were the deputy heads, and both were from the 'old school', being strict but fair. Our music teacher was Mr Gregory, and he would come round to everyone, putting his ear close to their mouths to make sure they were singing! Those of us who took packed lunches to school were allotted the music room as our dining area, and occasionally Mr Gregory would come in and 'serenade' us on the piano as we ate! Mr Lines took us for technical drawing, and he was

Somervale teachers. I think this must have been taken around 1960.
(Courtesy of Midsomer Norton Photo Booth Facebook Page)

also a strict disciplinarian. He once saw a pupil smoking in the street on a Saturday morning, and spent nearly 2 lessons the following week telling us of the dangers of cigarettes. It is amazing how these days we are constantly being told of the dangers of passive smoking, yet most of our parents smoked in the home without many of us youngsters taking up the habit. Many of our teachers smoked though, and you could smell the tobacco on them. Someone asked me recently if I could remember Miss Stark, who was our art teacher for a couple of years. She was young and attractive and smoked, but that was all I could remember! One master we knew for sure did smoke was the senior art teacher Tom O´Neill; he would retire to a storeroom in his class, and then come out releasing clouds of smoke! Maybe it was not unanimous, but O´Neill and Mr Jones seemed to be the least liked and respected of our teachers. Mr Voake took us for mathematics for a couple of years, and although this was my weakest subject, I was still disappointed to have got a D in my third year report, thinking that I had done that badly. I went to ask the teacher about it, and looking at my report book he realised a mistake had been made as my photo did not show me wearing glasses and he had mixed me up with someone else. There and then he changed my mark to a C! Mrs Duvall was our French teacher, and a very nice lady who unfortunately had to put up with unruly behaviour at times. Edna Duvall was actually born locally, and my father told me that she was his Sunday school teacher in his youth. Mrs Duvall was married to a Frenchman Aimé, and I believe the pair were decorated for bravery and services during WW2.

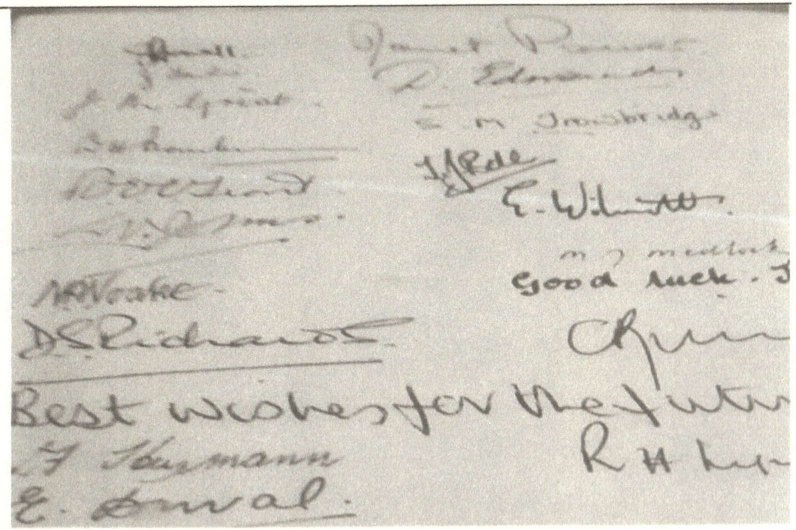

Somervale teachers signed our bibles.

Being in a school house was also something new to us, and in Somervale they were called after famous Britons; Blake, Drake, Colston and Scott. I was in Colston, and we seemed to be the last in everything, especially in Sports, which I think Scott excelled in, but at least we had Mr Barber as our housemaster. For the second term of our fourth year, we school leavers were put into class 5Y and made prefects. I think this was an innovation of Mrs Grist's who wanted us to act and behave as young adults, and we were even allowed to have our own coffee bar at break times. My job as prefect was playground duty; keeping order at break times. I would try to reason with anyone causing trouble, but if they chose not to listen then my partner Robert Smart would use more physical methods!

On leaving school, all the pupils were presented with their final leaving report, together with a copy of the New English Bible which we would get signed by as many of our teachers and friends as possible.

A mini Somervale reunion 1999 with Roger Coombes, Alan Jones, Phil Slater and Colin Maidment

I find it interesting to see the old photographs in the Midsomer Norton Past History Photo Booth Facebook page, and the members recollections of shops and businesses etc. During some of our art lessons at Somervale, we all went down to the High Street where we each had to paint a picture of one of the shop fronts there; the idea being that they could all be joined together later to make a long mural. Someone painted Gregory's sweet shop, I was given Dallimore's Cooked Meats, and others sketched The Palladium Cinema and adjoining businesses. On recent visits to the area, I found the abandoned cinema and the River Somer brook to be in a very sad state. It used to be a treat to go to the Saturday matinees at that cinema, and in the 4th year at Somervale we were taken there to see the classic film Ben Hur.

Site of what was Somervale Secondary School in Midsomer Norton

Teenage years

Becoming teenagers, you obviously start to go to concerts and shows to see your idols, and my friend Rob Beale and I went to see The Who several times in Bath Pavilion. On the way back from Bath there was no late bus to Stratton, so we had to catch one to Radstock and walk back from there, still half deaf from the tremendous volume the group generated. One night I said goodnight to Rob who lived at the bottom of the village, and carried on walking up to Bath View when a policeman on a motorbike stopped me, it being way past midnight. "Where are you going son?" he asked, and I replied that I was going home to Bath View, number 30.

"Ah yes," he said, taking his helmet off, "that is turn left in the estate."

"No", I replied, "it is up to the right." The constable seemed intent on catching me out, so next he asked me where I had been, to which I replied The Pavilion in Bath.

"What film did you see?" was his last question, but after putting him right that the Pavilion was not a cinema, he let me go on home, knowing what an upright law-abiding pillar of society I was!! It does show the difference though between those days and now, and how policing has had to change. Other concerts that our village arranged to go see were those of The Rolling Stones in Bristol's Colston Hall on two occasions, and Gene Pitney at the same venue.

My best friend Rob and I were crazy about music, and even tried to start our own group, but although we both had guitars, we never really learned how to play them, and were never able to afford amplifiers for them anyway. I was once given a piano accordion, a lovely old thing that was difficult to pick up, let alone play, but I had no interest in what I thought was a boring instrument, so tried to sell it. Just around the corner from the bus station in Bath there used to be a pawnbroker type of shop, which I think was called Knights. The owner was a not very friendly old man with a glass eye, and when I asked him how much he would give me for the instrument, he replied by asking me where I had got it from. I told him, so he advised me to "Take it back where you got it from son, I don´t want it!"

Robert was much more knowledgeable than me about music, and would always know about the new groups and singers on the scene. He had heard their discs well before they became popular, as he listened to the pirate radio stations Radio Caroline and Radio London. Before the pirate stations, Radio Luxembourg had been very popular, and much more interesting to listen to than the stuffy BBC stations of the day, the Light and Home programmes where new recordings had to share the wavelengths with studio-based musicians and orchestras. Who can forget the Horace Batchelor adverts on Luxembourg, with his plans for winning on the pools! "That´s Horace Batchelor, Keynsham, spelt K-E-Y-N-S-H-A-M-Keynsham, Bristol!" At least the BBC started to show programmes like Juke Box Jury introduced by David Jacobs. It was not until 1967 that Radio One was launched, with Tony Blackburn playing their first ever record Flowers in the Rain by The Move. Tony had been heard previously on both Radio Caroline and London.

Irish businessman Ronan O´Rahilly started pirate broadcasting in 1964, in competition with the monopolies held by the BBC and the big record companies. Like Dutch and Scandinavian pirates before him, this pioneer used a converted passenger ferry to broadcast from, and allegedly named it after President John F. Kennedy´s daughter. Apart from Blackburn, many well-known disc jockeys such as Johnny Walker, Simon Dee and Emperor Rosko started their careers on Caroline, while Radio London boasted Dave Cash, Kenny Everett and Ed Stewart amongst many others. These stations revolutionised British radio with their non-stop pop music and American style jingles. We would listen out attentively to hear the new records by The Beatles and others. BBC radio did have Pick of the Pops of course, and it was a must to listen to Alan Freeman on the show every Sunday afternoon. One of the first TV music shows I remember was Six-Five Special with Pete Murray, and then in 1963 ITV screened Ready, Steady, Go with Cathy McGowan.

I have not got the patience now to watch game shows, but as teenagers we were avid viewers of programmes like Double Your Money and Take Your Pick, with Hughie Green and Michael Miles. Until we got to an age where we thought they were corny, we were brought up watching shows such as Billy Cotton's Band Show and Dixon of Dock Green. How strange it seems to look back and remember how in those days we were able to watch almost all sport on TV without having anything extra to pay.

If you were not either a Mod or a Rocker in those days, at least you used to try to keep up with fashion, and we saw winkle picker and chisel toe shoes, Carnaby Street boots, bell-bottom jeans and rounded and button-down shirt collars come and go. When we started working we were able to catch the bus to Bath and visit Leslie's in The Corridor and other boutiques. Bath was also our favourite haunt on a Saturday night after the bars closed, and we would drive to the Taj Mahal Indian restaurant in Broad Street for a late-night curry.

That Hamlet on the Hill

Stratton village and Downside

Because of the presence of the famous Downside Abbey and public school in Stratton-on-the-Fosse, these establishments had a huge influence on the village. Downside own a lot of land in the village, and many local people were employed by them in many capacities, as were various foreign workers from Ireland, Italy, Spain and South America amongst others. Downside School is of course, the second largest Roman Catholic college in Europe, and as youngsters we knew of pupils there such as those of the Spanish Royal Family, and sons of actors Richard Harris and Rex Harrison, Mr T and musician Semprini. Although some of the Downside pupils were friendly and even came to our local Youth Club, in general we were not encouraged to mix with them and I am sure that they looked down on us to some extent. St Benedict's Roman Catholic School was also in Stratton during the 1950's and 1960's, before moving to Charlton Road near Midsomer Norton, and there was quite a division in the village between Catholics and Protestants in those days, although perhaps only on a social level.

One Downside pupil who certainly was not snooty was Bill Triggs. Bill was one of the college boys who helped create our youth club in Stratton Village Hall, and was a very friendly and down to earth person who got on well with everyone in the village. Some years later after leaving college, Bill returned to the area and married a woman from Stratton, the village he loved so much. Bill was related to the famous, fifteen times World Snooker Champion Joe Davis, and his brother Fred. I only discovered after his death, that the late Bill Triggs

Downside Abbey, Stratton-on-the-Fosse

had one of the world's largest collections of tenor banjo recordings, and a book of his was published featuring the songs of Harry Reser, a well-known player in the genre.

Downside School is now a mixed one, and I believe its grounds are more private and less accessible to village people than they were in our youth. We undoubtedly took liberties by walking on Downside land and playing on their tennis courts without permission, but things were more easygoing then, and the village cricket teams had been allowed to play on their excellent pitches for years. Many of our mothers or fathers had been employed by Downside in one capacity or another, and one perk of this was that we could attend the staff cinema showing on Monday evenings; we watched some great films there, even if the projector would breakdown on occasions. When a youth club was opened in the village for the first time in the 1960's, a few priests and pupils from Downside came to assist. Father Dominic, or Brother Dominic as he was then, was a magician and a member of the Magic Circle. We kids were invited to the school one day to watch one of his magic shows which was impressive, especially when he made a fellow monk ´float` up in the air from his bed!

Our Downside assisted youth club was held in the village hall, although the school also allowed us to swim in their large indoor pool at certain times, and occasionally invited us to their shooting range; teaching us older boys how to shoot rifles with live .303 ammunition! There was a rumour that the shooting instructor had a reputation for being ´over friendly` with the school cadets, so we village boys were a little wary when having to lie down and shoot at the targets! Mr Wells was a local butcher for the school, and had been an amateur boxer in his younger days, so as several of us were interested in this sport he offered to give us lessons. We made a makeshift ring in the hall, and Mr Wells provided us with gloves. As very often happens, one or two people always try to spoil things for the others, and on a couple of occasions a gang of rougher elements, led by someone who I could still name today, would come in and cause disruption. One night they threw some records belonging to one of the boys into a sink full of water, and gradually over the months the club lost members and interest. Strangely enough, none of the troublemakers offered to put on the gloves and take us on in the ring!

We village boys also played football against a joint Downside team comprised of pupils, teachers and priests. Dominic refereed a match on the day that I was reluctantly made goalkeeper, and saved what would have been a certain goal; the trouble being that it was not my hands that got to the ball but another sensitive part of the body. I ended up doubled over in agony, and as Dominic ran up to see how I was, one of the Downside boys said, "He got hit in the balls Brother!"

Another incident I would rather forget concerning Downside priests, was when I was riding down Green Lane on my sister´s bicycle, which was too big for me. I rounded a bend and encountered two monks walking abreast in front, and being uncertain what to do in that split second, shouted to them, "Out of the way!" I had instincively decided to ride on the inside of them next to the hedge, but on hearing me approaching, both men moved in and I rode straight into the back of one of them! Whether the priest was hurt or not I was not sure, but they were very concerned about me, even though I escaped with being only winded and having bent handlebars. Jokes about the poor men having 'dirty habits' or 'skidmarks' were not very kind!

Around the mid 1960's Downside had a very good rock band called The Benedicts, and some of us from the village were allowed to watch them perform in the school occasionally. Walking up the lane between the school and the cricket field we could often hear the group practicing or playing, and one day I climbed the wall to look over and fell, almost breaking my arm. I always remembered the name of the group's singer, and recent research showed that he went on to have a career in music and was a member of ELO in the 1970's.

Of course, many of the surrounding parishes were provided with catholic priests from Downside, and as I married a Spanish girl in 1972, I got to know several of them, even though I was still a Protestant at the time. I had to take an oath that I would bring my children up in the catholic faith, and we were married in St Benedicts church by Father Ambrose, who spoke fluent Spanish, and had been a missionary in South America. Along with Dominic, Father Joseph was assistant parish priest of St Hugh's in Radstock. Fr. Joseph gave me instruction when I changed to become a catholic several years later, and he was an interesting person who had also previously been Church of England, and an officer in the Welsh Guards. Coming from a famous brewery family, Joseph Coombe-Tennant once told me that he believed evil really existed, and that he had experienced things abroad during WW2 that led him to give up everything, including racehorses that he had owned, to join the monastery. Joseph must have been a least 6 feet 3 (1.90), and would fold himself into an Austin Mini to go visiting parishioners, until he suffered a hip replacement that is. One day Joseph came to bless a new house we had moved into, and while he was walking around sprinkling holy water, my young son asked me, "Will he do the airing cupboard too dad?" The Abbott of Downside Father John Roberts, like many C of E chaplains had too, saw action in the Second World War, and I have heard vague stories of him being a prisoner of war in Colditz. Certainly John was a man of the world who enjoyed a drink and a smoke. Midsomer Norton had a catholic priest around this time, whose name escapes me, but he was known as a bit of a tarter. If anyone spoke during mass, or if any children were making a noise, he would stop and stare at the guilty parties!

(Courtesy of DH James Photography)

There was also a convent of course in Stratton, and several of the nuns taught at the old St Benedicts catholic school there. Sister Angela and her companions ran a very strict establishment, if what our catholic friends told us was true.   Downside, like many religious institutions and individuals, has had its share of bad publicity and scandal in recent years, and this must have further alienated many people from the organised church.

A very disturbing story I heard of, concerned an episode that reputedly occurred in Downside School in the 1970's. I am not sure of all the facts, and by no means know if the story is true, but I did ask a certain school master about the affair one day in the Kings Arms pub, and he told me that it actually happened…The tale is that three or four senior boys had taken to playing with a Ouija board, which if true would have been seriously frowned on, and the pupils had summoned up an evil and violent spirit. Presumably this spirit was a particularly powerful one, and very dangerous, and there was only one priest profound enough to exorcise it, being as it had taken hold of the boys and of the room they were in. The account I was told of was that the exorcist spent several days locked in the possessed room, and finally had to strike a deal with the spirit to get rid of it, and this concerned taking the lives of the boys before they reached a certain age. A very dark story indeed, and one that I hope was just fiction.

Village institutions

In days gone by Stratton-on-the-Fosse had four shops, including the Post Office, and two drinking establishments. Now, 45 years after leaving the village, I believe only the Kings Arms public house still exists. This is a very old coaching inn; there is still a ring in the outside wall in South Street to which the horses were tied, and apparently a blacksmiths was situated just up the road years gone by. The Inn is in a corner position situated on the dangerous Fosseway Road, and during the time I was working there one evening as a part-time barman, we had a customer who had parked his car right outside the pub. PC Irving had taken over from Stratton's long time bobby Jock Macrae, and he was not as understanding as his predecessor. As the constable came into the bar and asked who owned the flashy car outside, the owner brashly said, "Do you not like my parking there?" To which Irving replied.

"I don't like it at all, move it now:"

The Kings Arms was run for many years by the Penny family, but not too many of the village working classes frequented it, as they were not really welcomed there. Dad would occasionally pop in there for a quick pint before going on down to the British Legion club, and he told me the tale that every time he gave Fred Penny a note to pay for his drink, the landlord would turn around from the till and ask if he had been given a pound note or a ten shilling one. Sure enough he was asked the same question one night, and dad replied, "It was a pound note Fred, serial number so and so," the one which he had noted and written down. It never happened again!

A man by the name of Hankin took over as landlord in the 1970's, and village people started to use the pub more, even though Mike was an old Downside boy himself. When I started working there some evenings and Sunday mornings, the pub was being run by Jeremy and Wendy Pook who were a very professional and businesslike couple. The Pooks attracted many local business people from the area, such as local butcher Dudley James and his wife, who was a teacher at St Gregory's School, and Mike and Jan, a couple who ran an estate agency in Midsomer Norton. The pub ran a successful gourmet evening on Thursdays which was well patronised. Jeremy was the chef, and before retiring to the kitchen he would smoke a pipe at the bar, but never before 6pm. Wendy's parents were Welsh, and her father shared the name with that illustrious prime minister Lloyd George. There was a lot of wit bandied about in the bar, and you had to stay sharp. One customer was looking through the menu, and asked Wendy what game pie was. "Clare?" was Wendy's one- word suggested answer, referring to the buxom girl who worked in the kitchen!

When the Pooks sold the pub I was asked to stay on part-time for the new tenant, who apparently had been an hotel manager in Bristol. He was Italian, and his wife was English, but what a change! As the landlord's drinking gradually increased over the months, so that he could hardly pass the optics without filling his glass, the business waned and custom fell off. Towards the end of his tenancy the only meals he served were 'steak sandwiches', which consisted of a piece of steak inside half a French stick, served with a carving knife from the kitchen!

I stayed on for my third landlord, who was actually a landlady. The brewery's strange choices now provided Stratton with an unattached divorcee. This lady relied mostly on her staff to run things, while she would make an appearance in the bar in the evening with her cigarette holder, fine nails and little dog. Behind the scenes though she had everything controlled, including written instructions made for the kitchen staff showing exactly how many leaves of lettuce and slices of tomatoes etc. were to accompany meals! How different from catering in Spain, where you often get free tapas! You certainly had nothing free at that time in the Kings Arms, and I am not sure for how long the business lasted, as I left working there soon after. It was sad to see the gradual decline of a good business, even though you could not really call it a village pub as such in those days. The pub did cater very much for Downside, and the masters, and even some of the priests, enjoyed the excellent real ales there in the evenings. Although I did not see him myself, the actor Richard Harris drank in the bar one night; I believe his son was a pupil at Downside, and Richard, a big drinker, caused quite a ´stir` in the pub, to say the least!

One unpleasant experience, that was a little embarrassing for me, occurred one evening when I was serving a young Downside teacher, who will remain anonymous, and one of the priests. The only other person in the bar was my father, who had popped in for a pint and a chat, and to buy me a half of lager. The three were chatting, and somehow their conversations turned to the war and politics. The teacher had been drinking quite a lot, and started to preach his pacifist views and his anti war sentiments. This incensed dad, and quite a heated row broke out before the kindly priest intervened and suggested his companion go home to his wife. Apologies all round followed, but I could have crawled into a hole!

I recall another sarcastic remark from a Somervale teacher, when he asked the class one day if any of us belonged to a youth club. I had replied that we had one in Stratton, and on his asking, explained that it was in the British Legion Club. I do not remember his actual comment, but it was something suggesting that we played the fruit machines there!! Along with neighbouring Coleford, the two villages ran very successful clubs, and customers would come from far afield to the Saturday night dances. Coleford club was a much larger one though, and in the 1960's were hosts to several big name artists who performed there. My friends and I saw such groups there as The Merseybeats, Them and The Pretty Things, although we missed Lulu when she also sang there!

Stratton club though had to content with local bands such as Ivor Hann's or Sammy Milsom's, but occasionally booked more 'modern groups'! The British Legion club was certainly the focal point of entertainment for many of the villagers, and Tony Perrett was an excellent organizer and secretary there during those busy years. Several ladies and mens skittles teams played there on the club's fine alley, and Stratton Legion also had teams in the local shovehalfpenny, darts and cribbage leagues. The club committee was made up of ex- servicemen, and the Rememberance Day parade was a large event in the village. The laying of wreaths on the war memorial followed an interdenominational service by the Church of England vicar and the Roman Catholic abbot, and then most of the congregation retired to the British Legion bar for well-earned refreshments!

Mrs Pratten was one of the club´s first stewards, and she was not amused to find that she had been serving some of us when we were still under 18! Bob Curtis and Pete Drew were also long serving stalwarts behind the bar. Children were welcome in the lounge with their parents, and us teenagers met up in the club for many activities. One year it was decided that we would build a float and enter the carnival, which was through Westfield at that time. The float was called ´Uncivil Defence´, and we were really just an unruly bunch in fancy dress. We had a stirrup pump on board, and someone thought it was a good idea to spray the crowds with water. An official complaint was made afterwards by someone who had gotten a soaking, with the result that a letter was received from the Deputy Chief Constable of Somerset, banning us from the next parade. The club did enter another float in the future, which was called ´Outer Limits` as the photo shows!

That Hamlet on the Hill

Possibly the oldest shop to survive Stratton village was the Post Office and Stores, although its location originally was a few yards further down the road, and which is now a private house. It was probably in the 1960's when part of the Frys Coaches office building was taken over by Doug Schmid and his family. Mrs Schmid was formerly Miss Fry, and a daughter of Charley Fry the founder of the business. Apart from running the post office and shop, the Schmid family were also proprietors of the petrol filling station, and for a while Fry's Bazaar.

Just around the corner from the Kings Arms stood Smith's shop. Harry Smith owned Smiths Bakery, which was quite a large business in its day, and they had a bread shop in Midsomer Norton's high street. The shop in Stratton though was more of a small general stores, and apart from Mrs Smith, I can remember Mrs Pawfrey and Mrs Mitchell serving us youngsters sweets on the way to school.

Stratton-on-the-Fosse Remembrance Day Parade.

Nearer still to St Vigors school was Mrs Taylor's shop, and in fact it was right next door to it. Mrs Taylor seemed ancient to us kids, and as far as I can remember she only sold confectionery. Sherbet dabs and jubilee bags spring to mind as some of our favourites, as well as chocolate bars such as Five Boys, Tiffin and Chocolate Cream. Who remembers Zubes pastilles that came in a nice tin?

The fourth shop in the village in those days was, of course, the one we called The Cafe. I am not quite sure of its history, but it belonged to the Stratton family of L and F Jones, who are locally famous for its string of retail shops, a wholesale cash and carry, and of course for owning the Centurion hotel and country club. The Cafe could possibly have been their first shop and business venture.

One other 'unofficial' establishment in Stratton was the Reading Room, run by Mrs Savage. Officially this was the snooker and billiards hall, and the table there was kept in good condition, as the village had teams in both local leagues. The Reading Room was the place where most of us village youngsters first started socialising, and apart from playing the table and card games, we could buy crisps, chocolate and coca colas there. Mrs Savage's talents did not end there though, for apart from running the rooms with a rod of iron, she also sold cigarettes, and took in punter's bets for the treble chance and the horses. Many a time our fathers would send us to knock on her front door with their football coupons, and to ask her for their packet of 10 Woodbines! These were innocent activities for a minor which would be frowned on today, but few of us were influenced to bet or smoke ourselves. Mrs Savage's husband Cyril was a chauffeur for Downside, and they had a son Alan. I can remember them all being heavy smokers, and 'Ma' Savage had a bad temper if you crossed her. She also had a sharp wit, and one day she was told by Michael S. that his sister had just had a baby. "What did she have?" she asked. Michael stuttered, but blurted out,

"T´were a- a boy or a g-g-girl."

"Well I never thought t´were a monkey," was her acid reply!

One regular visitor to the rooms was ´Scotchy` Dark, who unfortunately was the occasional victim of practical jokes, such as being locked in the toilets of the Reading Room. Scotchy had a bad temper too, but he was also Stratton´s cricket umpire, so if you had upset him somehow you would probably be given out early in the innings the next time you were batting! He was officiating one day at a match for the Downside Ravens, when he turned down an lbw appeal from their demon fast bowler. When the bowler was told "Not out," he shouted,

"How not?"

"Because I bloody well said not," returned Scotchy.

Neighbouring areas

Our nearest neighbouring villages were Chilcompton, which had a railway running through it and a ship named after it, and Holcombe, which had a park and tennis court! We had aunts and uncles in both villages, so we often visited both villages. A fond memory is of walking across the fields to the Holcombe Inn, later The Ring O´Roses, which was run in those days by the Denning family. Dad and his brother Uncle Jim would sample the local cider, while us cousins would play around outside and enjoy a bottle of lemonade with a straw and a bag of Smiths crisps, complete with a blue bag of salt! There was excitement one afternoon when a glider crashed into a field next to the pub. On occasional visits to Luckham Woods we would go to visit the old church in Holcombe, and entrance to St Andrews Church was from either through the woods, or via the lane and farm, where you had to request the church key. Legends tell that the site of this church of Norman and Saxon origins is where the original village was, and that the mound in the churchyard is where victims of the Great Plague were buried. St Andrews Church was rebuilt in the 16th century, and the churchyard also has a memorial to Captain Scott of the Antarctic, whose family once owned the brewery in Holcombe. I found out recently that there was also a factory in Brewery Road at one time called Wendy´s Crackers, where Christmas crackers were produced! As teenagers we held competitive football and cricket matches against Holcombe, and Chilcompton.

Left: Cousin Steve Seviour with Bobby Charlton. (Courtesy of Penny Seviour)

One famous footballer who had trouble finding Holcombe was probably England´s most famous player ever, Bobby Charlton. Bobby agreed to officially open the pub in the village and drove down to Bath from Manchester, after which he had no idea how to drive the rest of the 12 miles through the Somerset lanes. My late cousin Steve and his friend went to Bath to meet and accompany him back to Holcombe, as can be seen in the above photo. Steve did a similar thing with jazz legend Kenny Ball. Kenny and his Jazzman were playing at the Somerset Police Ball, which used to be held in the Downside gymnasium at one time. During the band´s break, Steve took Kenny Ball over to the Holcombe Inn to sample their cider!

Another ex England footballer who once came to Stratton to give a talk at St Vigors schoolroom, was John

Atyeo. Bristol City stalwart Atyeo was nowhere near as famous as Bobby Charlton of course, but he did score a goal in one of the few appearances he made for his country.

On the subject of personalities, a few were met in the Fosseway Club when they were guest speakers for the Lions or Rotary Clubs. One was England's famous fast bowler, the late (Fiery) Fred Trueman, who gave me his autograph in exchange for a large brandy! The story goes that Fred was staying at the Court Hotel at Emborough overnight, and caused quite a stir when he went home to bed! Another Fred who we met at the Fosseway was Wedlock, the local comedian who had a top ten hit with Oldest Swinger in Town. Perhaps the most interesting speaker I saw there was the author Leslie Thomas who wrote The Virgin Soldiers, which was made into a feature film starring Hywel Bennett and Lynne Redgrave, and The Magic Army amongst others. Leslie was very knowledgeable about several subjects, including cricket, and spoke a lot of sense, unfortunately though there were some hecklers present who just wanted to hear him crack jokes. I met Thomas while going to the loo, and he gave me his autograph on the back of my pay packet, dedicated to my dad who loved his books.

Not many well-known actors or actresses have lived locally, but some readers may remember a New Zealand born actor called James Laurenson who now lives in Frome. He starred in the Australian tv series Boney, and has appeared in many other British ones including Midsomer Murders, Bergerac and Inspector Morse.

Someone who may have been even more famous, and who lived in Holcombe at the time, was the actress Barbara Kellerman, star of such shows as The Lion, The Witch and The Wardrobe, and The Glittering Prizes. She also appeared in the war film The Sea Wolves with Gregory Peck, Roger Moore and David Niven. It is a fact that Barbara has one blue eye and one brown, but I never noticed that when I saw her coming out of The Hollies in Midsomer Norton one Saturday morning and approached her for her autograph! I always thought she was a beautiful actress, as well as a very nice person.

My memories of the Somerset and Dorset Railway and its station in Chilcompton are vague, although I can recall hearing the double engines struggling up the incline in the distance from Midsomer Norton. Locals could catch the train back to Chilcompton from town, then walk home the rest of the way to Stratton. Occasionally on a Saturday morning I would go to Chilcompton station with my father to collect birds that he had ordered from the magazine Cage and Aviary Birds. Although dad kept canaries and budgerigars, these ones he sent away for were more exotic breeds such as zebra and java finches. The birds would be sent out and delivered in small boxes with air holes in, and were watered and looked after by the railway staff. Unlike Midsomer Norton and a handful of other places, the site of the Somerset and Dorset railway station at Chilcompton has completely disappeared, although the famous Pines Express has places named after it locally.

Some of these miners were from Stratton too.

It is always interesting to visit the Midsomer Norton Station and railway to see what a fantastic job the volunteers have done in preserving it, and the news that they are extending the railway track to Chilcompton again is very interesting, although a video I saw on Youtube recently shows how difficult it will be to reach the Chilcompton Tunnel. The approach to the tunnel was through a deep cutting 40 feet deep and half a mile long, and this was filled in with waste after the line closed. One Christmas I was given Kevin Potts excellent book The Somerset & Dorset Line From Above, which follows the line from Bath to Evercreech as it is today by aerial photographs, and the filled in cutting and existing tunnel bores can clearly be seen.

Stratton-on-the-Fosse has to my knowledge only ever had one public house, but Chilcompton had 4 pubs that I remember; Naishes Cross, The Railway, The Brittania and

The Redan, some of which still exist, while some have disappeared or have changed their names.The landlord of Naishes Cross at one time was Mr Flower, and his daughter was in our class at Somervale School. Being the nearest pub to Stratton, by walking across the bridle path linking the two villages, this was the haunt of local youths, and also of older Downside boys who would risk being chased by the priests to taste the local beer. It would seem that there were even more pubs in Chilcompton in years gone by.

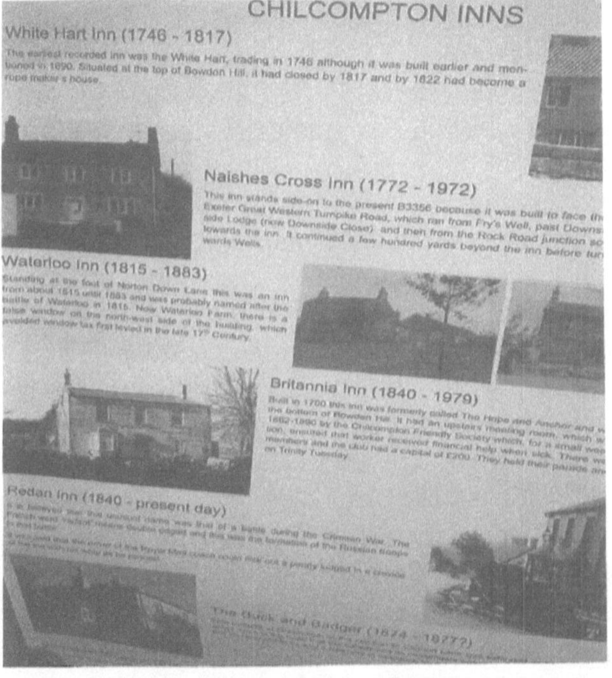

Left: Chilcompton pubs past and present.

It seems funny how we would say that we were going to, over, up to, into or down to a place, although there was disagreement over this. We would go *over* Holcombe or Chilcompton, *down* Radstock or Norton, *into* Bath, *up to* London or *to* Frome for instance!

That Hamlet on the Hill

The Mendips area, and Somerset and Wiltshire in general, have so many places of interest to visit that we were spoiled for choice on Sunday afternoon trips when the children were young. Weston-Super-Mare and Burnham-on-Sea were the closest seaside resorts to us, and many a winter afternoon was spent there looking out the car windows at the rain falling. Cheddar Gorge and Burrington Combe were great places to stretch your legs after lunch, and picnics at Chew Valley Lake and sightseeing at Wookey Hole Caves were also enjoyed. My favourite places to take the kids in good weather were Longleat House, Rode Bird Gardens and Stourhead Gardens. It was also a treat to visit the restored Steam Railway and Museum at Cranmore, and to ride on the miniature railway that used to be in Oakhill.

Near to Stratton and Oakhill is the village of Binegar, which also had a railway station in the days of the Somerset and Dorset. I was interested to read that up until 1955 there used to be an annual Country and Horse Fair at Binegar, and an account of this was written in the 1880's by Charles Hippisley Meade, who was born in the village. Around those narrow country lanes you also find Benter, and while, researching found that there are beautiful gardens to visit there in rural settings. The surprising thing to me was to find that one of the gardens is at Fire Engine House, so I presume that these are on the site of the old Fire Engine pub which we used to visit as teenagers. This pub seemed ancient even 50 years ago, and had no bar as such but just a drinking room and barrels of beer. As it was in a very out of the way place, the proprietor was not too bothered in asking you your age, provided you were with an adult. The adult in our case was Gerald Robbins, father of our friend Kenny, and with Rob Beale, the four of us would meet up at the Fire Engine for a pint. On the day in question Gerald arrived at the pub first and paid for 4 pints, which the landlord served and left standing on the barrels. For some reason though we three never turned up, so Kenny's dad was not very pleased with us and told his son later that he had to drink all the beers himself!

Mr Robbins had a good sense of humour though, and was a very nice man. As long as I can remember he drove a lorry for the coal board, the NBC, and one day he took Kenny and me with him to Portishead, where he delivered coal to the power station there. It was a murky, rainy day to add to the general miserable atmosphere there, and as we drove through the gates, Gerald frightened us by telling us to keep our heads down in case we were seen and sent to prison!

It is interesting to look back and see what occupations our fathers had, and quite a few of them in Stratton had either been miners or employees of Downside. Our Bath View friends were the Curtis' and their dad drove a large green furniture lorry which he parked outside their house. Other friend's fathers worked for Marcroft Wagon Repair Works at Radstock, at Showerings Babycham factory in Shepton Mallet, and EMI at Wells.

Before being employed by Clarks in Westfield, my father had worked for Ralph Blatchfords at their Wells depot, and on a couple of occasions he took me with him on a Saturday morning. Most of the workers there lived in the Norton/Radstock area, and they were picked up every morning by the Blatchford's lorry driven by Jack Francis. The lorry was a flat bed one with side flaps, and had a box shaped canopy where the men would sit. My memory of the works was of a mixed smell of diesel oil and cement, and there was also a large limekiln there. One chap who worked at the depot was called ¨White Rabbits`, presumably because he would do a spot of poaching in the surrounding woods! I was only eight years old at the time, but can remember seeing ´Old Harry` who worked at Blatchford´s, although he seemed to spend most of his time sat inside the shed. The story goes that Harry was frightened of the telephone, and that every time it rang he would call for someone to answer it. His exasperated foreman told him one day that all he had to do was to pick up the receiver and say who you are, so the next call that came in Old Harry lifted the phone and shouted down it, "WHO YOU ARE!!"

A nice gesture

The Royal British Legion, as it is now known, is not just about having branch clubs and putting on entertainment of course, and their poppy fund allows them to give tremendous assistance to people in need. I know my father, as an ex-serviceman, and my mother, both received help when they needed it from the Royal British Legion, and The Burma Star Association. The Legion played a different part in a rather fond memory I have concerning an old friend, Philip Gilson. Philip was a lot older than me, but as his wife and my then girlfriend worked together, we became good friends and visited them often in their house in Holcombe. This was the end house in Brewery Road, and by the time Philip eventually emigrated to Italy, he had been living in that same house where he was born for 60 years. Philip married late in life and had no children, and we would spend hours together chatting and drinking his cider. He had many hobbies including gardening, and a shed at the bottom of his plot contained a shortwave radio which he used as an amateur radio buff. His other big interest was pigeon racing, and although he did not keep birds himself, he would often go to Northern France with the lorry that carried them there to be sent off. This was usually at Avranches in Normandy, where Philip befriended a local family called Lebasac, whom we actually stopped off and met one year on our way to driving to Spain. Often Philip's wife Franca would cook for us and after, over coffee, would bring out a bottle of her marvellous Italian liqueur!

That Hamlet on the Hill

Franca Gilson was from Salerno in Italy, and she and Philip would go to see her family there every year, which included her mother and two nephews, one of which was a priest. There was serious fighting in Salerno during WW2, and the town has a large war cemetery for the Allied soldiers and airmen who lost their lives in that area. Almost certainly there is a cemetery for the Axis fallen too. Philip visited this cemetery on one occasion, and while looking around the church and its register, was surprised to find details of the grave of a young pilot from a village in Somerset. He was Flight Sergeant Knuttycombe, and he had been shot down and killed aged 22. Philip took photographs of the sergeant's grave, and on his return to the UK asked the British Legion if they could help locate any of the pilot's family that may still be living there. The outcome was that the boy's mother was alive, and still living in the same village near to Cheddar. She had never been able to visit her son's grave, and agreed to let Philip visit her. As Philip had poor eyesight and only used his car to drive to work at Coates Inks, he asked if I would drive him to see Mrs Knuttycombe one Sunday afternoon, to which I agreed. While Philip went inside to see Mrs Kuttycombe I stayed in the car, and apparently after being understandably upset, she thanked Philip gratefully for his thoughtfulness, and was very pleased to be given the photos of her son's grave, which she had never seen before.

A Great Train Robber in Stratton!

Another Stratton character who resided in Bath View when we were growing up was Bill Stevens. Bill was a storyteller and romanced a little, but no one knows to this day whether or not one of his tall tales was actually true. It was August 1964, and Charles Wilson, one of the Great Train Robbers, had just escaped from prison in Birmingham. Wilson was the treasurer, and joint organiser of the gang who had famously robbed the London to Glasgow train of 2.5 million pounds in 1963, and he was known as The Silent Man, as he confessed nothing to the police. A nationwide search was made for the escapee, and ports and airports were heavily guarded.

Our neighbour Bill told us kids that just around the days after the prison break, he was taking his dog for a walk early in the morning up Green Lane, which runs between the Downside playing fields. Green Lane is very bendy, and in summer has thick, high hedges that obstruct views. In the distance, and around one of these bends in the lane, Bill claimed to see a hearse stopped in a gateway to the field opposite the main cricket pitch, so keeping out of sight, he stopped with his dog and watched. His story related that the driver got out of his seat, walked around and opened the back of the hearse, removed the lid off of the coffin, and spoke to someone inside it!

We kids were very excited about this, and obviously went home and told our parents. Dad recounted the tale to his brother-in-law, my Uncle Eric Jones, who was a plain-clothes police constable attached to the transport police in

Bristol's Temple Meads Station. Eric duly informed PC Jock McRae, who was our village policeman and lived in Bath View. Constable McRae interviewed Bill Stevens, who apparently stuck to his story, unlikely as it seemed.

Presumably this information was passed on to higher authorities, but Wilson had disappeared anyway and was discovered much later living in Canada. It seems too fantastic that the famous criminal Charles Wilson had passed through Stratton-on-the-Fosse, and I wonder if there was ever a reward out for his recapture. What is certain is the fact that Charles Wilson was later shot dead in 1990 in Marbella, Spain, which is just down the coast from where I now live!

Stratton People Collection

Until recently, I had no idea that the Stratton People photo collection existed, and I was delighted to be given it on a CD. On the disc is a collection of photographs of Stratton people, taken probably in the 1950′s or early 1960′s by the well-loved Stratton photographer Stan James. All the photos were taken in very natural poses, and the collection of several hundred photos must have brought back nostalgic memories to the many people who have it in their possession.

Stan′s son, the late Doug James was also a very keen photographer, and he may have taken some of the photos in the collection too. Doug did in fact take the aerial shot of Bath View presented here, and he was the photographer for many weddings in the area, my own included. The company that Doug established, D.H. James Photography of Wells is still very much in business, and Nick James has very kindly given me permission to use some of his father's photos in this book.

Included in the selection are photographs of elderly people and youngsters from all over the village, as well as priests, nuns, teachers and the local police constable. Also of interest are the foreign people who lived in the village, apart from the ones who worked at Downside. Peter Willis and Mrs Carter were both German, and the war probably had something to do with their coming to live in England. There was also a Frenchman who lived in Stratton, and us kids would laugh and say that he ate snails! Apparently Mr Willis had been a good carpenter/joiner in Germany before the war, and I have also mentioned two Italian residents who were skilled as cobblers and barbers in the village.

Village football

Stratton F.C. Season 1922-23.
(Courtesy of Robert Beale)

My first recollection of watching Stratton United play football their famous sloping pitch, were of the players having to change in the old gasworks buildings nearby, and possibly people like Bob Burge, Alfie Smith and Alf Robertson were playing at that time.

Footballers were united in the '40s

MANY of the football players in this line-up of Stratton United in 1948 are still living in the area.

The photograph was brought to our offices by Pete Drew, who was only a year old when it was taken 55 years ago.

Some of those featured have died, one has moved to Australia, but most of them are still known to Mr Drew, who lives at The Willows in Stratton and works as a steward at the village's Royal British Legion Club.

Two faces he knows very well in the picture are the man on the left carrying a suitcase, and the boy in the dark jumper on the back row.

They are his father Pete, who died 32 years ago, and his brother Ron.

His father was the team trainer, and had his training and medical equipment in the case.

Mr Drew said: "I can remember every one of them and they were all village people.

"I used to help run the team in my teens and '20s, and the football ground where we played behind the gas works is still there."

The team folded some years ago, but there is still a village team in Stratton linked to the King's Arms.

Mrs Brady, near the end of the back row on the right, is in her late '90s and still living in Stratton, and her nephew Mike Brady, the young man standing at her right side, emigrated to Australia.

Pictured are, in the back row, left to right, Pete Drew, Margaret Dark, Dave Colbourne, Ken Read, Fred Dark, Leo Colbourne, Ron Drew, Tony Gould, Harry Stephens, Mike Brady, his aunt Mrs Brady, and Frank Beale.

In the front row are Maurice Atkins, Alf Robertson, Ray Cheasley, Ken Atkins and Trevor Bridges.

Ingrid Sofrin

STARS IN STRIPES: Members of the now disbanded Stratton United football team, taken during 1948, in a picture donated by Pete Drew. His father, Pete, the team's trainer, is pictured far left carrying the suitcase and his brother Ron in the centre of the back row

(Courtesy of Peter Drew.)

The team's goalkeeper in that era was, if I remember Rusty Wilkinson, but the village team had always been lucky to have had good goalies such as Tommy Wilson, Kevin O'Connor and others. Stratton United played in the Mid-Somerset league, which covered a large area, and included teams from as far apart as Wells, Cranmore and Bruton. In winter, we would be half frozen watching them play, and at home the red Stratton mud could not have been very pleasant for the players, not that is unless they were taking advantage of the downward slope! Many funny footballing stories have been recounted again and again over the years, such as when Lionel Dark refereed a game with a mouth organ instead of a whistle, and the day official referee Ginger Coombs booked a Stratton player who had been his best man and next door neighbour, asking him for his name under threat of being sent off. Bob Burge was playing full back in one game in which Stratton had already conceded several goals, when the opposing team´s winger approached him up the slope at speed. "Stop him Bob," shouted someone.

"No, let him have a shot," puffed Bob!

Stratton United team of the 1970´s. (Courtesy of Robert Beale)

The village also formed a Sunday morning football team which played in the Frome League as Stratton Old Boys, and were allowed to field two professional, or semi professional players. These players from Welton Rovers, Radstock and Frome Town such as Curtis, Margary and Kite, did not seem to mind at all playing on Stratton´s incline.

That Hamlet on the Hill

In the 1970's Stratton United had an excellent team, which was captained by John Alford, and under his leadership the side won several cups and leagues.

Stewart Seviour

Stratton cricket

A Stratton C.C. team showing the pavilion in the background.
(Courtesy of Matthew Western)

Downside's excellent cricket pitch was apparently laid by striking miners in 1926, and in 1934 it staged its only first class match between Somerset and Glamorgan. Stratton-on-the-Fosse first and second village cricket teams had, until recently, the privilege of playing their home games at Downside from July onwards after the pupils had broken up for their summer holidays. Having the use of first class wickets and a pavilion ensured that Stratton C.C. attracted the cream of local cricketers, but this also meant that few native village players made the first team. Even

Stratton second X11 had only a sprinkling of local men in their side in the 1960´s and 70´s, but I think that situation changed in in later years.

As I was cricket mad as a teenager, came from Stratton, and worked with fellow Clarks cutters Colin Francis and Terry Goodenough, it was natural that I befriended them and attended the club´s net practices. Colin was the captain of the village first eleven, and was an excellent opening bowler and useful lower order batsman. Connie, as he was affectionately known after the singer Connie Francis, was a tough competitor, and did not like losing. A lot of ´sledging` goes on these days in modern cricket, and Connie was not adverse to a little stiff rivalry with anyone who crossed him!

Terry Goodenough was also a very good strike bowler, as well as a powerful batsman. He had ´an eye` for the game, as most good all round sportsmen have. ´Goody` or ´Stone´ had a great sense of humour, and a love of music, especially that of Buddy Holly He shared my fondness for The Who, and once when we were fielding together he kept singing ´Pictures of Lily`, which was a hit for that group in the summer of 1967. Terry would also tease me at skittles when it was my turn to throw, by singing ´I can see for miles and miles`. Terry passed away much too early.

I had hoped to get a game of cricket, and thought that my chance had arrived when Stratton had three matches over a bank holiday weekend. In those days clubs announced their teams in the Somerset Guardian, but for those Saturday, Sunday and Monday games I was not even named as 12th man! I did finally get a chance to play when several of the regulars were away on their summer holidays, and felt, as a skinny bespectacled 17 year old, quite nervous before the match. To make matters worse, Dennis Moore came over to me in the dressing room and grabbed me by my collar, "Is it true that you have been f_____g talking about me?" he said, pushing his face right up to me.

"No, I stuttered, "that wasn´t me,"

"Oh, must have been someone else then," he laughed and put me down … My baptism of fire!

Dennis Moore and his post office co-worker Jimmy Parfitt were both important members of Stratton club for many years, Dennis being a reliable middle order batsman and slow bowler, while Jim was the team´s opening bat and wicket keeper. I was in the good books of Dennis when I took a catch off his bowling while fielding at gulley, although it was one of those lucky ones that pop into your hands before you know anything about it! There was an older player in the team Sid Filer, who would bring his father with him to the matches. Other players I remember were Derek and Terry Baber, Brian Norris and Martin Rumary. A few years later we were playing a game against a Somerset Ladies X11 and I was allowed to open the bowling against them, but although I tried my hardest, could not take any wickets. I did appeal for lbw once which the umpire turned down, and everyone fell about laughing as the ball had obviously not hit the batter on the leg, but clearly on another part of her anatomy!

It soon was suggested to me that I approach the second eleven, and I felt more at home playing for them, although that is not to say that they did not have some excellent cricketers in the team. In fact, one-time captain Ian MacDonald was a spin bowler of a class that you rarely see in club cricket. Ian was often a regular for Stratton first team, and any club would have been grateful to have him in their side. Ralph MacDonald was Ian's father, and a very keen cricketer for the Seconds too. Mac had been a manager at New Rock Colliery in Chilcompton. Don Rogers played cricket for Stratton second eleven for many years, mostly as captain, and other veterans of the team included Willy Grubb, Dave Read and Howard James.

Certainly Stratton had always fielded strong and successful sides in the period mentioned. Matches were played against teams from Bristol, Bath, Melksham and other adjoining towns and villages, and the highlights were the marvellous teas that most of the clubs provided, the best of all in my opinion being those of Avon Rubber C.C. of Melksham! Matches were also played against the Downside Ravens and the Somerset Wanderers Ladies, and a pint of beer never tasted better than after being in the field all the afternoon! Stratton teams have fared particularly well in recent years, especially since the advent of league cricket, but as of writing they have merged with Chilcompton, where they now play their home games.

Stewart Seviour

The story of a record player

One of our cousins from my mother's side of the family in Basingstoke, emigrated to Australia at the young age of 18; this would have been around 1964, and when he left home my Aunt Peggy gave his record player to my older sister Pat. In those days of course 45's, or vinyls as they are now referred to were what young people bought and played, and the number of 'singles' sold each week contributed to how the hit parade, or top twenty was fashioned. At one time a single cost seven shillings and sixpence (about 0.38 pence), and we usually liked a record played on the radio enough to buy it, although new releases from groups such as The Beatles or The Rolling Stones were often purchased before even being heard, and still went straight to number one in the first week

When Pat married and left home, I took possession of the record player. More modern radiograms were in fashion, and as well as being a piece of furniture, they were a unit where LP's and singles could be played, as well as featuring a built-in radio. Luckily she left the collection of singles for my brother and I to enjoy, although the player had seen better days by now, and it was not long before the stylus wore out and so we bought a radiogram too.

Stratton United with first aid kit!

While still single, we youngsters followed Stratton's football team, and several of us who were not actual players in the village contributed instead by being committee members. A trainer was needed for the team, but in those days that did not refer to a coach or manager, but rather to the lower position of 'bucket and sponge man!' Although I had no first aid knowledge except for the absolute basic, I was asked to take on the role, which initially just entailed running onto the pitch to douse a winded player with the freezing cold water! Stratton United were playing in a cup final however one day when defender Mark Schmid was injured and bleeding, so I realised that I would have to get myself some sort of first aid kit, and this is where my old record player came in! I stripped everything out of the casing, cleaned it, and painted the team's name on the outside. Filled with bandages, plasters, Germolene and other healing properties, the case had a new lease of life, and was photographed with the team!

Left: record player turned into -   Right: first aid case!
(Football photos courtesy of Stephen Beale)

That Hamlet on the Hill

Part-time jobs

It was common for some of us to make pocket money by having a morning or evening paper round, or by delivering milk for instance. I was never fortunate in either of those respects, but when I was thirteen, Stratton resident Ted Mabberley asked my mother if I would like to have a Saturday morning job delivering bread for Steam Mills Bakery with him; Ted had two other local boys helping him for the last few years, but each left as they reached fifteen and started work. The pay was seven shilling and six, which rose to ten shillings for my second year. Ted was well respected and straight as a die, but our age gap showed when he told me that his previous assistant had been able to save his wages and buy himself 'a sports jacket and a pair of flannels.' Mr Mabberley had previously been a coach driver for Frys Coaches, and is was reputed that he would sulk if he did not get to drive the newest coach, or bread van.

Starting at 7.30am, we would drive to the bakery in Midsomer Norton and load the van with bread and cakes for a shop in the High Street, before returning again to load up for the bread round, where I had to hunt around for a decent wicker basket and leather money bag. The round started at Chilcompton Road, and then on up to Norton Down and White Post before proceeding to Stratton, where we would stop for lunch. The afternoon took us to Stockhill and Chilcompton, and I would spend a lot of time waiting in the van for Ted who seemed to have some favourite lady customers! My Auntie Olive was one of our customers in Bennell Cottages, and whenever I saw my cousins Jenny and Jacky they would tell me that when Ted called on them he would nearly always have a runny nose, and this would fall on to the cigarette end he inevitably had in his mouth. Not very appetising, to say the least. I was not very popular with one lady, who lived in a private bungalow, but for a different reason when I carried her small hovis to her

one day in my hands; she told me in no uncertain terms to take the bread back, and to bring her another one 'in your basket!'

In summer it was hell in the van with the wasps everywhere trying to pitch on the cakes, and I must have killed dozens of them by squashing them on the windscreen with a cloth. Ted would always let me take home some cake when we had finished the round at about 4.30pm and this usually meant a whole custard or cream slice that the wasps had been at, and which Ted called, 'That bloody mess!' What a great variety of breads there were in those days and maybe still are; bloomers, cottage loaves, pound and half pound, split, procea, brown, and of course sliced. As for the

delicious cakes we sold, lardy, traffic lights and cream horns were my favourites. We also delivered bread to some of the prefabricated houses that were erected at New Rock Colliery in Chilcompton, and which housed the families of the Durham miners that had came to work in the area in the 1960's. Coalmining is documented as being carried out in Stratton-on-the-Fosse, Clutton and High Littleton in the time of Henry X111, and was part of the local coalfields which later included others at Benter and Nettlebridge. New Rock Colliery was sunk in 1819, and closed down in 1968.

Dave, a neighbour of ours, worked underground at New Rock for a time, where he befriended some of the Durham men. One Saturday a trip was organised by them to Southampton to see the Saints play Manchester United, and I was invited. The North Country miners were a friendly lot, and big drinkers, and I got the chance to see the likes of Bobby Charlton, Denis Law and George Best play!

That Hamlet on the Hill

**

Starting work

Regretfully like many pupils who left school at age 15, heedless of the advice of their teachers and headmaster, work for me started at Clarks shoe factory in Westfield, Radstock, where my father had been working since 1958 or so. It was not because we were forced to leave school and find a job, more so that we were just not encouraged to stay on and study. Neither did I regret working in the factory at the time as the pay was good, even if it had to be hard earned. Looking back though it was foolish to start one´s working life so early and not to have studied for some qualifications; thankfully years later my own children were still at university in their 20´s. As with many other manufacturing trades, shoemaking is a thing of the past in the West Country, although Clarks St. Peters factory must have been a very welcome employer when it opened in 1956. An innovation too was that the company held annual Christmas parties for the children of employees!

Children of St. Peters employees Christmas party.

In a nutshell, the factory received the raw materials, the uppers were cut and then stitched, the soles were vulcanised on, and then the finished shoes were packed in boxes and taken away by the big green Clarks lorry parked up to the loading bay. Between those basic stages though, scores of different operations were carried out by the several hundreds of employees.

I heard by letter that I had been accepted on probation by Clarks, which meant that new employees were on trial for three months to see if they were to become satisfactory workers. Straight after the two weeks summer holidays I commenced my working life in August 1965, right at the bottom of the heap as repair boy in the Making Room. This was the department where the shoes were soled and finished, after coming from the Closing Room. In those days the men in the Making Room worked three, eight hour shifts, mornings from 6.00 to 14.00, afternoons from 14.00 to 22.00 and nights from 22.00 to 6.00. Some workers were on day shift however from 8.00 to 17.00 with an hour for lunch, and these were the hours in my contract, the same as those worked by the women in the Closing and the men in the Cutting Rooms.

The Personnel Secretary in St Peters at that time was Dilys Smith, working under David Simms, the Personnel Manager as he was called in those days. Dilys married Colin Wall, who was on the staff of Clarks, and we get to see them most years on their winter holiday breaks to Málaga. Dilys has a remarkable memory, and we have reminisced many times over the old days.

Vulcanising operation

We nervous new recruits were introduced to our heads of department, given some vouchers to spend in the canteen (wages were always paid a week in arrears so we had to wait ten days for our first pay packet), and told that we would be subject to a medical examination by the works doctor. I think there were around ten of us new workers, but the only two I can remember now were Colin Maidment and Jimmy Higgins. Like mine, Jimmy's father Harold also worked in the factory, also on vulcanising. These operatives would look after several vulcanising machines which melted the rubber, then shaped the soles of the shoes on to the uppers, being the leather components stitched together. The uppers were put on metal lasts the same size that the shoe was to be, and then placed in the vulcanisers, which were similar to large ovens that gave off tremendous heat.

The heat and noise of a factory are the first things that hit you, but the most unnerving thing for a newcomer must be to have to walk through the length of the whole factory with hundreds of eyes seemingly on you. After a few days at your own workplace though, you begin to settle down and to recognise familiar faces. The Making Room was no paradise however, some of the operatives were a hard-boiled bunch, and did not take to fools kindly. Many operations had to be carried out, and the work was transported all around the room on conveyor belts. These men were on piecework and their speed was something to behold. The operations ranged from tacking the cardboard insoles onto the uppers, roughing the leather edges prior to vulcanising, to 'finishing off' and trimming the spewed rubber. At the end of all the operations the finished shoes were examined, and as Clarks quality standards were extremely high, those not up to standard would be sold as 'jobs' or sub-standards.

Colin Maidment remembers that before becoming a cutter, he too started off in the Making Room as a general dogsbody. Recalling how innocent a recruit he was, one day he was being taught box making by an operative he knew well and came from his village. When it came to this man's morning break-time, he told Colin to have a go at the job while he was in the canteen, and he was getting on really well for half an hour until he realised that he was doing his friend's piecework for him!

As the makers were on piecework, it was inevitable that mistakes were made or faults found, and it was basically my job to go around the line to collect shoes that had to be unpicked and corrected.

Half a ticket, or tray of six pairs of shoes.

A toothcomb was used to pull out the tacks all around the bottom of the unsoled shoe, and if the fault lay with the Closing Room it would have to be taken back to the woman who did the repairs in that department, who in turn would take it back to the operative responsible for the faulting stitching or folding. The repaired upper would then be taken back to the Making Room to the relevant worker. This had to be done quickly as shoes were always made as a ticket, which meant 12 pairs, and the whole ticket would be held up until completed. I quickly found friends with Stuart Mitchell, who took me under his wing to teach me the job, and Terry Prior from the other shift was just as helpful. I preferred working with Stuart´s shift, not just because I could go and have an occasional quick chat with him, but because I got on better with their foreman Joe Edgell. The opposite shift seemed to me to have more 'hard types`, but the main reason was that I did not get on very well with Joe's counterpart Sid Paine. Sid was an older man who had the reputation of being grumpy, and seemed to be on my back most of the time, but he was just doing his job and everyone had their superior to report to.

The same lack of motivation and ambition that made me leave school early, led me to be happy enough working where I was, which would have meant eventually progressing to work on the line. Thankfully though, decisions were taken for me in that it was decided that I had potential to work in the Cutting Room, so I was informed that I was to be given a cutting test. After three months or so as a repair boy I was not really keen to be changing departments, but was encouraged by everyone that it was a good move. The test showed that I was not colour blind; a very important attribute when having to match shades of leather, and the examiner must have been satisfied that I had aptitude for the job involved as the test was passed and I was to be transferred as soon as a vacancy arose.

The Cutting Room was regarded as somewhat of an elite place to work in, and although in a way it was an apprenticeship, as you had to learn the skills of cutting, at least you were working dayshifts and not tied to a conveyor belt. In the mid 1960's some of the older cutters like Ivor Cook, Ray Mears and Dave Mitcham still wore a collar and tie with a white apron. The ultimate goal was to become outside cutters like them, which meant that you actually cut the leather uppers for the shoes and boots. In those days though it could take a youngster five years to become one of these top paid operatives, and you had to work your way up by way of being first a fur lining, and then a lining, cutter.

Clarks St Peters cutters reunion 2010 at The Crossways Inn.

Jeff Hodder was one of the few persons who actually worked on the line in Making, and had also been a cutter. During a cutters reunion in 2010 we spoke about the differences between the two workplaces and Jeff commented, "To me the main difference was that the cutters had more camaraderie. Even though the job was just as cut throat, the cutters would stick together more, probably because they were all doing a similar job. Out of work, the cutters also tended to meet up more socially.

I have searched on the web on occasions for descriptions of cutting or ´clicking` in footwear factories, but the only reference I found, likened it to cutting out pastry shapes as you do in cooking. As far as cutting fur linings for boots or shoes goes, this is not a bad description, but in the case of cutting leather or synthetic materials however, the ´knife` is the metal shape that has a sharp cutting edge. These knives are heavy, and are the exact size for the component you wish to cut out of your material. Fur lining material came in large rolls which you placed across your cutting block, and unlike leather, several layers of it could be cut at the same time.

The term ´clicker` apparently came from the original presses that were used by the leather cutters, and these had a large beam that you swung around and positioned over the knife, after which you pressed the two knobs to make it come down and cut out your pieces. These presses made a clicking sound. Later on, most of these machines were replaced by more modern German - made presses called Moenus, which had push button operation and were much less prone to breakdown. The cutting block was actually made of four wooden squares with a hardwearing synthetic surface. The 4 blocks fitted together, and had to be changed around weekly so that the surfaces wore evenly and prevented a depression from appearing in the middle. If this happened the knife could break, and so just enough pressure had to be applied on the beam. Too little meant that the cut was not deep enough, and too much could drive the knife into the block, causing damage to both, and earning a bollocking from your foreman!

A very old clicking press & knives.

The lining cutters were very skilled and could earn good wages, and in most cases they were waiting for a vacancy to arise to become an outside cutter. The linings were made of natural materials which had flaws in, and care had to be taken to cut good quality pieces, even though these ended up on the insides of the shoes. For this reason the skins had to be inspected and cut up individually. As mentioned, shoes were made as a 'ticket' which were twelve pairs, and these stayed together as a unit all through the various processes of the factory. In the case of a cutter, he would receive his job of work as a bundle of skins of leather, and he would have several 'tickets' of work to cut which could comprise of different sizes and width fittings of footwear, such as 10C or 12A etc. Clarks Shoes of course were the pioneers in introducing width fittings for their footwear.

A more modern Moenus cutting press.

Both outside and lining cutters earned their wages by the same basic method in that they had a certain time allowed to cut each ticket of work, and the total 'minutes' earned were calculated at the end of the payment week. What made the job special and skilful though, is that the operatives earned bonus for leather saving. Skins of leather were measured to a quarter of a square foot, so you could be allocated say 100 square feet to cut up your total job, and if you only used 90 then you would be paid bonus for saving 10 feet of leather. Skins of leather were graded depending on their quality, and on the amount of it that was usable to cut shoes out of. If the quality of the skins were poor, then the cutter would be allowed more footage with which to cut out his uppers.

A whole animal hide is large, so it was cut in half down the backbone so that the cutters could manage the skins better on their cutting block. Being a natural material, leather has many imperfections such as marks and scratches caused by insects, or by the cow rubbing against barbed wire for instance. There were also holes in the leather, and soft, stretchy parts in the areas of the animals neck and legs. The best parts of the skins were from the backbone down, and it was from this area that the vamps, the front parts of the shoe, were cut. These components had to be cut tight to toe, so that the uppers did not stretch when later operations were performed on them. Good leather also had to be used for the outside quarters, or the piece running right around the outside of the shoe. If you imagine a shoe for your right foot, the piece down its right hand side is the outside quarter or outside counter, whereas the left side piece is known as the inside quarter. These inside quarters could be of inferior quality, the reasoning being that they are not as visible. Softer parts of the leather could also be used for the tongues or tabs.

Among the cutters skills then were cutting the important components out of the best leather, working fast to make his minutes, and cutting tight to save as much material as possible. This was done by pushing into the smaller or inferior areas of the skin where the vamps could not be cut, and by running in with the smaller tongue or heel knife. The older, more experienced men tended to cut slow and waste little leather, whereas those of us with young children and a mortgage to pay worked faster! It was not an easy thing to get the right balance with good quality too, but that was what was expected of us.

At any stage of the shoemaking process the partly, or fully, completed shoe could be rejected due to the cutters fault. Mostly this would be caused by a flaw in the vamp opening up into a cut when it was stretched. If the upper had not yet had the sole put on it, then the flawed part would have to be cut again. However, quality inspectors at the end of the production line could discard sub-standard shoes for poor quality cutting, and this would result in the pair of shoes being declared a job lot, traced back to the relevant cutter, and shown to him by his foreman. In the early days of the factory's life, operatives were actually fined for any sub standard shoes they produced. Rows of lovely shiny products in a shoe shop window would be spoiled if the products had cuts or other deformities in them.

Of course, such a complex system of payment and bonuses necessitated a large and efficient Wages Office.

The development and planning of new lines of footwear was also carried out in St Peters, and the cutters would normally be shown the model of a new shoe. This invariably led to disputes, as they were often unable to earn the same pay as they had on older, established lines. If this happened, and a deadlock occurred, a trades union official was sent down from headquarters in Street to meet with a Clarks trouble shooter, but if still no agreement could be reached it was not uncommon for an official, or unofficial strike to be called. Our main representative from the union was the man with the unfortunate initials Vic Dyer, and it was often felt that he sided with the management rather than with his members! I came to the conclusion though that strikes never benefited the workers in the long run, as management always had the upper hand, and could always take back any concessions they had made one way or another.

As the quest for better quality products was sought, incentives and quality leagues were set up, where the manufacturing departments were in competition with one another. The eventual league leaders won a departmental prize, which normally consisted of a night out. On one occasion our cutting room celebrated their league win, courtesy of C&J Clarks, at Birnbeck Island in Weston-Super-Mare. On another occasion in the 1970's our department went on a trip to London, and a group of us drove there in a hired minibus. The plan was that we would meet up again in the evening for our meal, but would split up into groups during the afternoon for different activities. Two of the options were to either watch a football match at Loftus Road between QPR and another London team, or seeing some of the Saturday Ashes play at The Oval. To my everlasting regret I chose to watch the football, and missed the chance to see that great Australian team which included Dennis Lillee and the Chappell brothers! Winners or losers, we enjoyed a few beers, and I remember us country bumpkins having difficulty with the London Underground system on the return journey to our meeting point!

Quality League Winners Cutters celebration!

Social life

Most employees in the factory joined in social occasions, and we cutters always organised Christmas and other parties, either in local pubs, or at nightclubs such as The Webbington. These nightclub visits often got rowdy towards the early hours of the morning, but on one occasion a major incident was only just averted. After supper, some of our members had wandered downstairs to the club´s heated swimming pool, where a group of local rugby players were enjoying a dip. Due to the wine and the atmosphere, words were exchanged, and before anyone knew what was happening, one of our party was thrown into the pool, complete with his suit on. As poor R was fished out of the water and taken upstairs to get himself and his clothes dried, it looked as though a big fight was on the cards, and one in which we would have come off second best. By now some of the older members of our party had arrived and were trying to calm things down. Rex Hughes was most vocal, and someone said, "Yeah, let Rex have a go at them, he fought the Japs in the war!" What Rex did though was to throw the clothes of one of the rugger players in the water, to which they accepted as a detente, and we all left the scene unscathed..

St Peters had a very active skittles league, both ladies and gents, and with two divisions to cater for the shiftworkers. Some of the very best players entered teams for the Leathermark Trophy, which was a competition made up of teams from all the Clarks factories in the West Country, such as Weston-Super-Mare, Shepton Mallet, Minehead and Bath; there was a lot of travelling involved, and competition was very sharp. St Peters skittles teams all had their own home alley in a local pub, and memorable nights were had at such places as the Faulkland Inn, Nettlebridge, the Dolphin at Welton, and the White Hart at Midsomer Norton.

The Young Generation Clarks Skittles team with trophies.

As a newbie who was playing his first game that Friday, I remember asking Ivor Cook what it was like at the Crown Inn at Clapton. His sardonic reply was that it was ´Waaarm ´n dry.` Apart from normal league games that were held on Friday evenings, cup competitions and knock-outs were organised. After the match, those who had ordered supper would enjoy their bread and cheese and pickles, or faggots and peas, and then it was the custom to hold a game of westbury or coffins, with everyone trying to win the money we paid into the pool. Westbury was a game where every player who had entered threw their three balls, and the money went to the one who had made the highest score. With coffins, each player entered threw one ball, and if he or she failed to hit a pin they lost their life. The last player standing took the money.

At the end of the skittles season in April or May a presentation dance was held, usually at the village hall in Farrington.

Skittles trophies from 1972 season!

Prizes were awarded to the league and cup winners, and also to the players who had made the highest individual score as well as the highest spare. For anyone not familiar with the game of skittles, a player's throw is to roll three balls at the pins, and he has six throws. If he hits all nine pins down with either his first or second ball, then the skittles are stuck up again for him. In principle a player could score 27 in one throw, and this has been done often enough. A variation of skittles we played was nomination, which meant that you had to nominate and call out the pin you intended to knock down. I discovered that there were other variations of skittles played in different parts of the country, such as Devonshire skittles where the player throws the ball with both hands, and ends up full length on the floor! In the Bath league, I was surprised to see that when one team were having their throws, the other side retired to the bar until it was their turn, then vice versa. That would have spoiled our league as a lot of good natured barracking went on between teams and fellow workers.

Several teams from St Peters entered themselves annually in The Norton Sixes cricket competition, which was held at Midsomer

Norton cricket ground, and we even held a Rounders League for a few years, which we also managed to win one year.

Fishing trips were also arranged and enjoyed, but things did not always go exactly to plan, such as on the day we went mackerel fishing to Beer in Devon. Four of us went out in a small boat and caught nothing, but the worst thing was that the outboard motor kept faltering, and conked out. Ernie Coates got it working again, but instead of steering back to shore he headed out further to sea for better pickings. When the engine stalled a second time, we waved at some other boats nearby who waved and shouted back at us! Water was also coming into the boat, so we frantically waved our shirts and baled out what water we could, until eventually someone towed us ashore, where we bought some mackerel in the town to take home with us. A deep-sea fishing trip to Weymouth on Norman Fishlock's boat was no more successful, and all I came back with was a case of severe sunburn!

Our winning Rounders team!

Running a General Stores

It must be the ambition of many people in their lifetime to run their own business or to become self-employed, and several workmates over the years had taken the plunge and left their jobs to run pubs or to become builders etc. Workers tended to get stuck in a rut, and unlike nowadays, it used to be possible to spend your whole working life doing the same job for 50 years or more. Many people toyed with the idea of buying a bar in Spain, or a fish and chip shop somewhere, and there were no shortage of property magazines advertising businesses, and ones which were usually run down or not viable. Obviously money is needed to start any business, and on reflexion, if you have it, then why buy yourself work and worry!

If you are intent on doing something though it is not east to be deterred, and the fact that the new manager of Lloyds Bank was reputably keen on helping people set up their own businesses in the area helped us take the plunge. The corner shop we bought in Midsomer Norton´s Redfield Road was The Crossway Stores, and in hindsight, the days of small shops was way past. The former proprietor had a lot of good customers, and we got to know some very nice people like next door neighbours Molly and Lily Hill, and their sister younger sister Jacky Collins who lived next door again. Old Mr Batt and Mr Turner would call in Saturday mornings for their cakes, and whilst most of our neighbours would pop in for odds and ends or bread, there were one or two customers who would give us their weekly orders, such as Mrs Paget, whose husband owned the Paget Press, and we would deliver their groceries to them. Mrs Prior of Priors soft drinks company, and Mrs Chivers were two ladies who would come in regularly to have a moan, but apart from a little shoplifting by school children, it was a pleasant experience. Some of the customers who had bought a lot of shopping with the previous proprietor had done so on credit, so we lost most of them.

That Hamlet on the Hill

As it was close to Christmas when we took over the stores, we were introduced to, and invited by several wholesalers to their stock presentations, such as Humphries and West, with the intention that we would give them our orders. Stock had understandably been run down in the shop, so a large order was given to wholesalers Moffats for sweets, chocolates and cigarettes. There is little profit in cigarettes, and as in petrol and fuel, most of their price is made up of taxes. At the end of the month this stock had to be paid for, whether you had sold it all or not. This did not exist with general groceries however, as we used Jones Cash and Carry, or occasionally other wholesalers farther afield. It was amazing the number of deliveries even a small shop had, and they included Steam Mills just around the corner, and Paul Denning of Clandown for bread and cakes, Hales for boxed cakes, Pullins Dairy for milk, and another Pullins deliveryman called with other products such as cream, yoghurt, cold meats and pies. Hughes Bros. delivered our fruit and vegetables, and also potatoes which we would weigh up in 3 and 5 pound bags. Cheese we would buy in blocks, mild and strong cheddar, and it was my job to use the cheese cutter to prepare a selection of pieces of each, wrapped in cellophane of different weights and prices. Care had to be taken with the cheese, as it could soon start to go green if kept in the cooler cabinet for too long. We had a disappointing experience on one occasion. which was through no fault of our own, but it lost us a customer nevertheless. The local cricket club had started to buy a few things from us for their teas, convenient for them as we were just over the road from them, but one day they had to return a jar of strawberry jam which had black mould on the top of it when opened. Although the stock was new and we apologised, the damage had been done.

Right: The Crossway Stores.

After leaving full time work to concentrate on the shop, ways to improve trade were looked into, including enquires about the possibility of selling newspapers. Dave Parsons from Parsons Newsagents was a customer of ours who called in every morning for his brown loaf, and he advised me that it would be very difficult to get a supplier for papers, as this type of business was a very controlled one. Dave did give me some names to contact though, and the outcome was that I was given a franchise with a supplier to sell Sunday newspapers; this was very welcome as we had quite a good Sunday morning trade as a convenience store. The papers and magazines were on a sale or return basis, so it was a good addition for the shop.

Customers had from time to time asked if we sold beers or wines, and I was already thinking about applying for an off licence even though there was already one at the other end of Redfield Road, and the Crossways pub was also just opposite us. I put in my application, and in due course a notice arrived in the post with a summons to appear before the Magistrates Court in Radstock. This was the first, and so far only time I have been in a courtroom, and when I saw several local landlords, including those of The Crossways and The Kings Arms milling around, naively thought that they were there to block my application! After a few common sense questions however, my application was approved and I was granted an off-licence. The pub landlords were there of course to apply for some sort of mutual extension of opening hours.

We also had a delivery every couple of weeks from Corona, for their lemonade, orangeade etc. These crates of soft drinks were kept in a small outside wooden storeroom, and on one particularly cold morning all the bottles had frozen solid and cracked. We also found a huge rat in the storeroom one day: believe me that are hard to catch, but after a short battle I managed to corner and finish it off with the broom handle! In those days there were no rules and regulations governing when and where you could deposit your rubbish and glass etc. and a shop had to get rid of a lot of cardboard boxes and cartons. We used a small incinerator to burn our waste, but like garden bonfires, I would imagine that this practice has long since been banned!

Voluntary redundancy

By the late 1970's and early 1980's trade was irregular for Clarks, and the firm suffered from cheaper competition and changes in styles and customers tastes. Through this, the factory suffered quite a lot of short time working, and the cutters were affected by this as much as anyone. Often our foreman would come round on a Thursday to tell us, "Half day tomorrow," and sometimes there was only enough work for a four day week. The consequence of this was that the company offered voluntary redundancy to anyone who wished to take it, although there were some cases that were compulsory. Several long-term cutters took the opportunity to leave for various reasons, and many started up and ran their own retail businesses, such as fruit and vegetables or fish and chips. One or two ex employees also set up their own off-shoot businesses in the leather trade, mostly manufacturing belts and handbags.

A handful of cutters 'moonlighted' for Mulberry of Chilcompton, the now world famous fashion accessories firm, and they helped set up the company in their early days by cutting out the leather bags and belts from a small shed in the village. It is common knowledge of course that Mulberry was set up by Mrs Saul and Roger Saul, the wife and son of Clarks factory manager Michael Saul. It seemed a natural progression that some of these very experienced leather workers should eventually set up their own firms, and did so successfully by such ways as obtaining contracts to make belts and holsters for firemen etc. I was not very popular one day while I was part-time cutting for Mulberry and suffered an accident, as it caused some embarrassment. Most of the work was hand-cutting, which meant that we cut round the patterns with a hand-held knife, rather than the pieces being cut out on a mechanical press. Stanley knives and blades were the normal tools used, but some workers preferred to make their own knives out of filed and sharpened hacksaw blades. My knife slipped on this occasion, and sliced off the tip of my left index finger, causing my companion Pat to nearly faint! Our foreman Keith Porter drove me quickly to hospital in Bath, where a skin graft had to be made on my finger. The injury still occasionally gives me pain and problems 40 years later, but at the time it meant that I was off work from my main job, due to an accident suffered at my part-time one. When I went to see the Personnel Officer I was told, "We know how it happened, we all know how it happened!"

So it came that Christmas 1981 saw an exodus of workers from Clarks, myself included, much to the wrath of my bank manager who had given us a mortgage on the shop on the strength of my job! After 16 years working in a factory it felt strange, but good to be free and not having to be on piecework and looking at the clock, although it soon became apparent that the shop was not going to support a family. We eventually sold the Stores, but not until I had started a couple of interesting, but poorly paid jobs. On my last visit to Midsomer Norton it was sad to see that Casswells, the famous hardware store, had closed after so many years, especially as I had worked there briefly.

Casswells were much more that just a hardware store though, they even had their paint shop in a separate location, just opposite on the corner of the Island, and which I remember being run by a quiet chap called Paul. The main shop where we worked sold almost everything you needed in the way of bricolage and do-it-yourself, with the adjoining one selling household appliances and fixtures and fittings. Outside was the builders yard, leading to the bathroom and kitchen centre. Casswells was very much a builders merchants too, and I learned that many local builders, plumbers, electricians and other tradesmen used it extensively. Most of these tradesmen bought on credit, which meant that we filled out invoices for the goods and materials that they had purchased, and their accounts were then sent to them for settlement at the end of the month.

Particularly interesting was learning about what the plumbers asked for in the way of pipes, joints etc. I was soon able to go to the stores unaided to fetch what they wanted, whether it was a Yorkshire joint or a stopcock, and got to the stage that I even had to advise them what they needed sometimes! I had a good teacher in Don Ashman, who had run his own hardware shop for many years in Westfield. Don was a Methodist lay preacher, and a very nice man with a great sense of humour. Mike and Dave also worked in the shop, and to say that they had a wicked sense of humour was an understatement. Everyone worked hard though, and there was very much a sense of the seasons of the year, as the window dressings and goods on display had to be changed around for Spring for instance, with the seeds and garden tools. Sorting out and displaying seed potatoes was another big seasonal job, and in those days, many people still grew their own vegetables. Sometimes we would have to help out in the builders yard where the customers would drive in to buy bags of cement or sand, or other materials. Steve ran this yard, and the firm employed a full-time driver for deliveries.

It was either in the yard, or the tearoom, where you would usually meet the father and son who worked together, and who were a always a bit of a mystery to me. The pair drove a lorry, but it was never clear to me if they were actually employed by Casswells, or worked for themselves. Apparently Casswells had a store or arsenal somewhere nearby where detonators and explosives were kept, presumably for use in quarries, and as far as I knew the two men were licensed to handle and transport these items. Pete was the general manager of the shop, while Mike and Simon ran the bathroom centre. The fathers of Pete and Mike were two of the three directors of the firm, the third being Mr Hobbs, whose own son once ran a Gun and Sports shop in The Island.

That Hamlet on the Hill

The family who bought Don Ashman's hardware shop in Westfield later started up a non-food cash and carry warehouse in Coombend Radstock, which was called Tradeware. Apart from being a centre where local businesses and small shopkeepers could come to buy goods in bulk, Tradeware also had a very successful delivery service, with their three vans delivering orders to places as far afield as Swindon and Chippenham. Through my visits to the warehouse I got to know Brian, one of its co-owners, and he offered me a job as warehouse foreman, a fancy title maybe, but a diverse and responsible one which I became proficient at, dealing with Persil Automatic, toilet rolls and Christmas gift sets amongst hundreds of other goods. The warehouse was large, and in winter was the coldest place I had ever worked in, with only a big oil-fired turbine affair as heating. There was plenty of physical work to keep you warm though, and pallets of the various lines were brought from the goods-in storeroom to the main warehouse where I would place and arrange them. A box of Ariel or Persil or similar would hold 16 packets of washing powder, but sometimes the customer would only want half a box so you would find the space between the packets and split the box in half with your knife, taking care not to cut

Former non-food Cash and Carry in Coombend, Radstock.

open any of the packets. You then had to work out half of the price of the box, add so much percent to it for the privilege , and write the amount on the remaining half. A good system which gave a little more profit. It was necessary to help out occasionally with the unloading of the goods from the massive delivery trucks that called every day. The yard was on a steep slope, so care had to be taken when driving the forklifts with pallets of heavy goods. Washing powders were extremely heavy, but cases with jars of jam even more so, when a few lines of foods were introduced, including wholesale chocolate and crisps. Now, this is another local business that has sadly closed down.

That Hamlet on the Hill

Crossroads

In the nearly five years since some of us took redundancy, the St Peters factory was, with a reduced workforce, busy with work again. They actually advertised for experienced leather cutters, so I swallowed my pride and applied, and was granted an interview which proved successful. I was not the only worker to return, and we were soon accepted back by our mates and settled in. Although our foreman was the same person, there had been changes such as a new factory manager, and the actual physical location of the cutting room had been changed around to where the making room had been. There was plenty of work to start with, and we were even on overtime, which usually meant working an extra hour during the day starting at 7am instead of 8am, or on a Saturday morning. Even though we were on piecework, Saturday morning working was a more relaxed atmosphere, and hours were flexible as long as we worked our four or six hours, so most men started at 6am to have as much as their weekend free as possible. The good days did not last long however, work became short, and once more we found ourselves on short-time and loss of wages. It was getting more difficult to adjust to the regime of factory life again, and a quarrel over a quality issue led me to hand in my notice a second time.

Disillusioned at being tied down to a machine and rejected for a staff position, my wife encouraged me to try to get employment in sales, despite being 39 years old. An advertisement announced that individuals were required for some sort of sales – training, and hopefuls were invited to a presentation and interviews in a Bath hotel. The person who answered their phone number was quite ambiguous about giving information, and would only say that the work involved using "visual aids!" On arrival, all the applicants and curious were given a black, imitation leather folder, which I think I still have somewhere, and inside were reading and instructional material. When the talk and presentation commenced, it soon became obvious that the business was about selling financial services, namely savings plans with life cover, and pension plans. Those of us who retained our interest in the job, which would be more on a part-time basis to begin with, were asked to attend further training courses the following week. The courses were quite intense, and selling was going to be fierce and competitive, with the aggressive type of training that companies such as Allied Dunbar used in those days. One of the main visual aids taught us was to draw figures of the family we were trying to sell to, showing the father and mother as perhaps joint breadwinners, and then smaller figures as the child(ren). Next, we would ask them what their total income and expenditure was, and what provisions they had made for life insurance and pensions. This nearly always gave us the opportunity to tell them that they would be struggling to maintain their present lifestyle if one; and here we would strike out the diagram of the father, or other of the parents should unfortunately die. They would be advised that the level of insurance cover they held at present would only last them x number of years, and that they should seriously consider increasing it, or be starting a savings plan!

So, armed with our sales material and recently required knowledge, we were let loose on the public, with the company's high hopes of our success. These days 'cold calling' is not allowed, but that is just what we were expected to do in 1989. Our initial program was to contact five or six of our close friends or relatives, and to make an appointment to go along and see them, not necessarily to sell to them, but to practice our new skills and ask them evaluate our performances! That was a good idea, but when it came to actually having to pick up that phone and ask a close friend, perhaps one you had not seen for years, if you could call around and have a chat with him about your new position in sales, then your courage nearly leaves you! However I left family out of it, and only one acquaintance turned down my request for an interview telling me in no uncertain terms to get lost! Appointments made, it was then the hardest thing in the world to get out of the car, and to go and ring your friend's doorbell. Things got easier though once you were inside their home, and had explained that you were moving in a different path in your career, and that you were just 'practising' on them. Tea or coffee, or a drink was usually offered, and then one lesson that we were taught was shown to be true, that one or other of the couple prove to be the dominant one and asks the questions, so you direct your presentation at him or her, while the passive partner listens. As with all jobs of course, experience brings confidence, and when you finally make your first sale it is a fantastic feeling, even if the commission is small, and at the end of the day a private pension or savings plan is a product well sold.

They say that everyone reaches a crossroads at least once in their lifetime, and that the decisions you take at that time can influence your future life. After working part-time for a local broker and achieving some success, I knew that I could communicate with people and was enjoying selling, so decided to apply for a full-time job in the industry with Prudential. Unfortunately my application and interview proved unsuccessful, the reason being that I did not seem to be outgoing enough, so rather despondently decided to continue in the leather trade. Within a couple of weeks though, Pearl Assurance were advertising in the local paper, stating that they were interviewing candidates for the position of district agent in their Bath branch, so my wife encouraged me to apply.

On the morning of my interview I came home from work early to change into my suit, but then had cold feet and changed my mind! This was my first crossroads; I was nagged and told that I should be sensible and go to the interview, and the eventual outcome was that I spent the next 26 years in the insurance industry! I was given the usual tests, questions and answers, and forms to fill in, and a few days later I received a phone call from Branch Manager John Stevens. He too told me that I did not seem to be the usual outgoing or aggressive type that the company would normally employ, but because of my age and mature attitude he was prepared to give me a chance. Basically this meant that I was to be sent on Pearl's two week training course in Peterborough, and if I passed out, would then be employed on a three months probationary period.

The position of District Agent was that the successful candidate would be given an area of Bath or Bath district, where he would carry out his duties in the IB or Industrial Branch. IB agents called on customers in their homes, and collected their premiums in cash for whole life or endowment policies, and were expected to sell new policies to existing and non-existing clients. Remuneration was part salary plus commission, with some expenses and benefits. Industrial Branch policies had been written in the UK between 1854 and 1994, so when I started my training in 1989 things were already beginning to change.

Pearl's complex in Thorpe Wood Peterborough was very modern and pleasant, and most of the candidates shared a bedroom with one other. There were two of us from Bath, which was C16 Division, and part of the Western area under an Area Manager, who I believe was based in Bristol. Applicants were from Divisions all over the British Isles, and I only met two or three who were older than myself. Jeremy from Swindon was my roommate, and we helped each other with the studying and swatting for our exams, which were quite intensive.

It soon became clear that the job entailed more than we had thought, and there were at least eight products that we had to learn and be proficient about, and then be tested on during the second week of our course. Each policy product at our disposal had different terms and features that needed to be learnt inside out, even though we would probably only be selling 2 or 3 of our favourite ones, and these included savings plans as well as insurance policies. A welcome surprise was that we were also allowed, and expected, to sell GB or General Branch business which included motor, home and commercial insurance. We also were given several training sessions on bookkeeping and accounting, as Pearl´s systems were quite complicated to say the least, but we had to have them

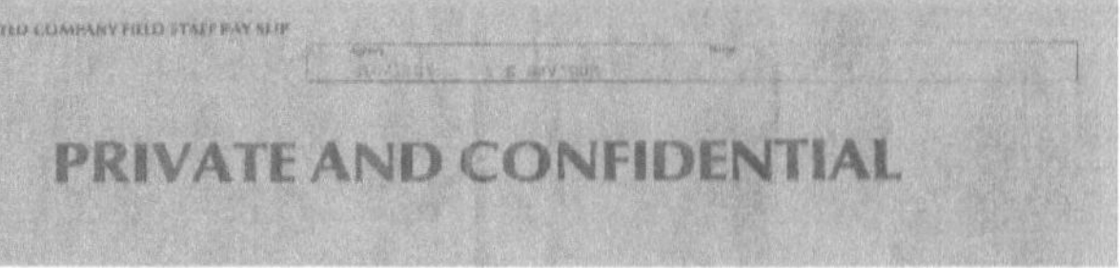

My first payslip!

ready and in order to present to our Branch Manager at the end of each month.

Apart from having to study hard, the course was very enjoyable and the food and accommodation excellent. There were also moments of fun, such as when we were each filmed on video practicing mock-ups of selling to an imaginary client. The videos were played back to us and discussed and rated, and if our performances did not make us cringe, then our regional accents did! Tyson was the other person on the course from Bath district, he was only about 20 years old and had a real cockney accent. When doing his roleplay on camera Tyson struggled to get his briefcase open, and then he kept referring to his client as a pundit! Unless you were very unsuitable or unintelligent, the tutors worked hard on any individuals who were struggling, and the majority of applicants passed the course successfully at the end of the second week. Relieved, Jeremy and I had good marks, and the following Monday I presented myself at Pearl´s office in Bath, where I was told that I after training I would be taking over the Odd Down agency and their book of business.

There were something like 16 agents based in the Bath office, and these were split into two sections each with its Section

Manager, and covered Bath centre, north of the city and on to Chippenham, and our section which covered south of Bath and out into the country areas, Norton/Radsock and Stratton-on-the-Fosse. Roy was our direct manager, and for my first two weeks he accompanied me on my rounds, introducing me to my customers, and teaching me hands-on everything I needed to know. Roy had many years experience with the company, and had an easy-going and pleasant personality that endeared him to customers and colleagues alike. He would tell me anecdotes and stories about fellow workers, such as the agent who owned a Robin Reliant and who had a large rat run in front of his three wheeler car one day. Obviously feeling it was safe to be between the wheels of a car, the surprised rat got squashed by its front one! "Gotcha," said the driver! Entering competitions and crosswords was one of Roy's hobbies, and he told me that he had shelves upon shelves of reference and information books. Apparently he entered nearly every competition he could, and had won several prizes that included foreign trips.

All payments had to be carefully entered in our agency ledger, which was our "bible", as it had details of all of the agency's customers, and could be scrutinised and utilised for finding new leads and increasing existing business. When doing our rounds and collecting premiums, we were taught to always be aware of new opportunities for business, whether it was encouraging the customer to take out new policies, or asking about other members of their family. One system that worked well was to go to a library and look at the electoral roll for your area, and then find the names of young people who were going to be eligible to vote for the first time. A request would then be made to their parents, and often they would give us permission to speak to their son or daughter with the object of selling them a pension or savings plan.

It was part of our responsibility too to find leads for our OB or Ordinary Branch Inspectors, one of whom accompanied us every few weeks or so. OB differed to IB in that it was for larger contracts and policies that were set up on direct debit, and which is the norm these days. We were expected to find 2 or 3 good, or warm leads for these inspectors, and in my case they came along with me on a Monday evening. These men were expert at their jobs and could earn high commissions, and while we learned from them, they in part relied on us agents for their leads and income. One of the very best was Tony P. who must have been near retirement age, but was still hungry and successful and would only write good and solid business. After one not very successful Monday evening, Tony and I stopped for a drink before going home. It was at the top of Brass knocker Hill or somewhere similar, and we could look down across Bath with all its lights glittering, and Tony said, "All the thousands of people that are living down there, if only we had a guiding hand to tell us who to call on."

If only indeed!

Quite the opposite to Mr P. was an inspector G, who was young and had a different approach, but usually topped the sales charts each month. Unfortunately, a proportion of the business he wrote did not stick, and the next day the customer would cancel the proposal that he felt he was pressured into signing! Of course, this meant that the commission the OB man had earned for that month, would have to be paid back the following one! This applied to us agents too of course, as we would receive a percentage of that commission. Often when calling on a customer again, they would tell us not to bring THAT inspector round here again please! Dave was my favourite companion, and we worked well together as he was another easy-going personality, and was attractive to the prospective clients. He once told me that when he was younger he tried on a couple of occasions to join the police force, but was turned down even after doing well in his interviews and tests. On asking the reason for this, a recruiting officer took him to the window and asked him the colour of a car that he pointed out. Dave got it wrong, he had red-green colour blindness. Another young salesman, whose name fortunately fails me now, was a bit kinky and liked his wife to dress up in a nurse's uniform! Nothing wrong with that of course, but it was rumoured that he liked heavy breathing!!

On occasions our Branch Manager would accompany us on an evening round, and apart from finding him some warm leads, we would also have to be on our best behaviour in front of him. Actually Mr Stevens was a good and fair boss, who always had the door of his office open to everyone, with the stipulation that you knocked first before entering. He told me that when we were alone he was John, but when in front of clients I was to address him as Mr Stevens. I had started the job at the beginning of July, so it was a bit embarrassing to tell John that I had a holiday to Spain booked for 2 weeks at the end of the month. We had our ferry crossing booked to drive down through France and Spain to visit my wife's family, but I was given permission to have the time off, with a friendly reminder to work twice as hard on my return!

Transport

My first experience of driving on the continent was in 1975, after crossing to Northern France, and encountering thick fog at about 5am. Driving slowly, and last in a queue of cars following each other's tail lights; unfortunately the lead vehicle was going in the wrong direction, so we all turned around, and I now found myself in front of a few other stragglers. I was driving nearly blind, and had no idea where I was going, but kept hearing a whoop, whoop sound, which turned out to be the Granville Lighthouse. We were that close to the cliff top…. and they say that you do not learn to drive until long after you pass your driving test.

Most of us youngsters started off our driving experiences on a motorcycle, and my first one was an old James 200cc which my dad bought from Mr Parsons in Coombend, Radstock, and then I had a BSA C15. Not for me a first-time driving test pass, it took me three efforts at Wells before being able to tear my L plates up. The next logical step was to learn to drive a car, and unlike here in Spain, I was able to practice if accompanied with a full licence holder. I fancied a black and red Mini I had seen in a garage in Glastonbury, and although it had seen better days and had holes in the floor, was what I could afford. The dealer arranged to take my BSA in part exchange, and I rode there one Saturday morning with my brother-in-law Rodney on the pillion. The motorbike was on its last legs too, and I was glad to get shot of it as it had a very bad oil leak on one side of the engine, so Rod suggested that I park the bike with the leaky side against the wall. We duly signed the papers and set off towards home, but coming up the steep hill out of Wells the car started to overheat, so after letting it cool down we drove it back to the garage where the owner was preparing to close up until Monday morning. After promising to have the car roadworthy for us by Monday afternoon, he apologised that he had no vehicle to lend us to drive home in. Then, you guessed it, he said, "You can ride your motorbike back again though!!"

Left: My first car and girlfriend (later wife!)

One of the most popular driving schools in the Norton/Radstock area at that time was the Three R′s, which was run by Rex Ruddock who had possibly worked at Clarks before my time. Rex encouraged learners to be confident, and to put their foot down when circumstances allowed. I was not feeling very confident at all when having the one hour drive with Rex before the first of my two tests, and to show how nervous I was he said to me after we had pulled up, "Bloody hell young′un, I′ve never seen anyone do that before, you changed from fourth to first gear all in one go!" I passed my test the second time at Wells in December 1969, but not before the examiner had politely asked me if I would like to attend to my windscreen wipers. It was raining at the beginning of the test, but when it cleared up I was concentrating too much on my driving to remember to turn the wipers off, even though they were grating on the windscreen!

Everyone seems to have tales to tell about their driving test experiences, and one of the funniest I heard was when a candidate was told by the examiner to turn left. The left indicator in the car was broken, so the driver asked the examiner to put his hand out for him! That situation would not arise in Spain though, because when you take your driving test there are two or three other learners in the car with you, and you all stay inside while each of you takes his test. That would be enough to make anyone nervous, and it was nerves that prevented my father from passing his motorbike test on several occasions. On the day he finally did pass, he had been caught up in an army convoy driving through Wells, and took a long time riding back to where the examiner stood. Strangely enough though, he said, "Pull in here Mr Seviour," and passed him, which was a relief to the rest of the family as poor dad had a habit of coming home, throwing down his helmet and saying, "Bloody failed again!!"

Dad's bike was only a modest BSA Bantam, but in those days several teenagers rode high-powered machines such as Ariel Leaders and Arrows, and later on, the even more potent Japanese bikes. Youngsters from Stratton had their share of accidents too, some of which sadly involved fatalities and serious injuries.

That Hamlet on the Hill

Going back

People say that you should never look back as we cannot make the past return, but we all feel nostalgic at times, and like to turn the clock back. We started the Stratton-on-the-Fosse Facebook page in 2013, and it now has some 275 members, many of whom have posted interesting old photographs, articles and personal recollections. Midsomer Norton are also very active on Facebook with their Past History Photo Booth.

Places and buildings unfortunately do not always stay the same, but there is always an interest in returning to see some of the homes we once lived in. Our first home when we married in 1972 was in Waldegrave Terrace in Radstock, which was a two up and two down old miners cottage with a huge garden sloping up the hill. We bought the house and got a mortgage from Norton Brokers, who had refurbished and modernised it. I have not been back to that street for years as it was always so difficult to turn your car around there, although you could, with practice, reverse smoothly into a neighbour's drive. We had some very nice neighbours in Waldegrave Terrace, most of them elderly people who had been living there for years like ex miner Gilbert Norris, and Mr Kemp, who told me that he was a former engine driver for either the GWR or the S&D Railway.

It is sad when places you knew, or worked at, have disappeared or changed completely, and on a recent visit I found it hard to believe that the area around the former Clarks shoe factory was so different now, and that the old Elm Tree pub has been demolished.

The site of the old Number 30 Bath View.

The biggest surprise to me was to find out that Bath View in Stratton no longer existed, as most of the houses there had been demolished to make way for a new, modern estate of houses and bungalows. Comparing the site now, it is not easy to imagine where our old rank of houses stood with the drive leading up to the row of garages, although one of the Smiths houses can be seen in the background.

How a junior typewriter got me to Spain!

Due to family links and love of the country, I was thinking more and more of emigrating to Spain by the late 1990´s, and although I was very happy working in insurance, the cold weather and the rat-race of British life was making me yearn for a change, and like thousands of others, looking for a better quality of life and a better environment for children to grow up in. Industrial disputes, strikes, rising mortgage rates and constantly moving house and changing cars, all contributed to my wanting to start afresh. We already owned a small property in my wife´s town in Badajoz, and although being on holiday is not the same as working in a country, I started to think seriously about trying to make a living in Spain.

While working for Clarks I had tried unsuccessfully on a couple of occasions to get a transfer to their Portugal factory, but realised that I was not suitable material for a staff position with them. Although being very grateful for the training and experience that Pearl had given me, I set about finding British insurance companies who were operating , or had branches in Spain, and wrote to five or six of them on my daughter´s junior Silver Reed typewriter. We still have the typewriter today 26 years later, and it was gathering dust in the attic until I took it down to take a photo of it!

That Hamlet on the Hill

Left: The magic typewriter!

Within a couple of weeks I received replies from two of the insurance companies, and they both offered me interviews in Madrid on the same day, Sun Alliance at 8am, and Royal Insurance at 9am! This was in January 1991, and in the middle of the first Gulf War, so both Heathrow and Madrid's Barajas airports were full of armed police and troops with tanks. When we flew from the UK there was snow on the ground, but it was nowhere near as cold there as it was in Madrid. The Spanish capital is higher above sea level that any other in Europe, and you needed a glass of Rioja to warm you up! Royal Insurance had told me that they were looking for an English-speaking inspector in their Málaga branch, and although my insurance experience and Spanish language was not as broad as I had hinted, I must have influenced them as I was given a second interview with them to meet the manager and staff in their Málaga branch.

It suited us to fly to Sevilla and hire a car for the drive to Málaga, where we were met with lovely warm, Andalucian sunshine. After the interview and introduction to the office staff, we were given instructions to meet an agent of Royal who could rent us an apartment until we got on our feet. I had been coming to Spain at that time for nearly 18 years, but on the drive to the Costa del Sol I caught my first glimpse ever of the Mediterranean Sea! We were shown an apartment in a building where we later purchased one, and we still live in it 27 years later. After we returned to Somerset, it seemed strange to receive a phone call at 8am from Royal Insurance, but of course they were one hour ahead of us and was 9am there. To my relief I was offered the job as a Commercial Inspector for the Costa del Sol, so we had a month or so to partly tidy up our affairs. This was not the second crossroads in our lives, (that came later on for me) as we were all looking forward to emigrating to Spain and it was a conscious decision. All that is except our son, who thought at the time that we were going to a ¨third world country`, although he soon liked it well enough!

We had started an adventure, but no one could foresee that the future would bring redundancy, owning our own business for the next 20 years, and managing to run a cafe bar in between times. I also reached my second crossroads, but that is a story to be told in my next book!

Other titles by Stewart Seviour

www.ingramcontent.com/pod-product-compliance
Lightning Source LLC
Chambersburg PA
CBHW022217050726
47590CB00002B/843